THE RUSSIAN REVOLUTION
AND BOLSHEVIK VICTORY

Why and How?

PROBLEMS IN EUROPEAN CIVILIZATION

UNDER THE EDITORIAL DIRECTION OF

Ralph W. Greenlaw* and Dwight E. Lee†

DECLINE AND FALL OF THE ROMAN EMPIRE — WHY DID IT COLLAPSE? †

THE PIRENNE THESIS — ANALYSIS, CRITICISM, AND REVISION*

THE CORONATION OF CHARLEMAGNE — WHAT DID IT SIGNIFY? *

THE GREGORIAN EPOCH — REFORMATION, REVOLUTION, REACTION? *

INNOCENT III — VICAR OF CHRIST OR LORD OF THE WORLD? †

THE RENAISSANCE — MEDIEVAL OR MODERN? *

MACHIAVELLI — CYNIC, PATRIOT, OR POLITICAL SCIENTIST? *

THE REFORMATION — MATERIAL OR SPIRITUAL? *

THE CHARACTER OF PHILIP II — THE PROBLEM OF MORAL JUDGMENTS IN HISTORY*

PROTESTANTISM AND CAPITALISM — THE WEBER THESIS AND ITS CRITICS*

THE ORIGINS OF THE ENGLISH CIVIL WAR — CONSPIRACY, CRUSADE, OR CLASS CONFLICT? *

THE REVOLUTION OF 1688 — WHIG TRIUMPH OR PALACE REVOLUTION? †

PETER THE GREAT — REFORMER OR REVOLUTIONARY? †

THE GREATNESS OF LOUIS XIV — MYTH OR REALITY? *

THE EIGHTEENTH-CENTURY REVOLUTION — FRENCH OR WESTERN? †

THE ECONOMIC ORIGINS OF THE FRENCH REVOLUTION — POVERTY OR PROSPERITY? *

METTERNICH, THE "COACHMAN OF EUROPE" — STATESMAN OR EVIL GENIUS? *

THE INDUSTRIAL REVOLUTION IN BRITAIN — TRIUMPH OR DISASTER? *

1848 — A TURNING POINT? *

NAPOLEON III — BUFFOON, MODERN DICTATOR, OR SPHINX? †

OTTO VON BISMARCK — A HISTORICAL ASSESSMENT*

THE "NEW IMPERIALISM" — ANALYSIS OF LATE NINETEENTH-CENTURY EXPANSION*

THE DREYFUS AFFAIR — TRAGEDY OF ERRORS? †

THE OUTBREAK OF THE FIRST WORLD WAR — WHO WAS RESPONSIBLE? *

THE RUSSIAN REVOLUTION AND BOLSHEVIK VICTORY — WHY AND HOW? *

THE VERSAILLES SETTLEMENT — WAS IT FOREDOOMED TO FAILURE? *

THE ETHIOPIAN CRISIS — TOUCHSTONE OF APPEASEMENT? *

THE NAZI REVOLUTION — GERMANY'S GUILT OR GERMANY'S FATE? *

THE BRITISH IN INDIA — IMPERIALISM OR TRUSTEESHIP? †

THE OUTBREAK OF THE SECOND WORLD WAR — DESIGN OR BLUNDER? †

THE COLD WAR — IDEOLOGICAL CONFLICT OR POWER STRUGGLE? †

Other volumes in preparation

PROBLEMS IN EUROPEAN CIVILIZATION

THE RUSSIAN REVOLUTION
AND
BOLSHEVIK VICTORY

Why and How?

EDITED WITH AN INTRODUCTION BY

Arthur E. Adams

MICHIGAN STATE UNIVERSITY

D. C. HEATH AND COMPANY · BOSTON

Table of Contents

Introduction

THERE are several warnings to which anyone proposing to study the Russian Revolution must listen before setting out on what is certain to be a fascinating but perplexing intellectual expedition. It is essential first to understand that this revolution was an incredibly complex historical process. Acted out on a nationwide stage it presents an almost limitless panorama of suffering humanity caught up in a series of swiftly evolving crises no one seemed able to prevent. Passions and pressures built up through many generations of frustration were concentrated in a social and political upheaval that may be likened to a long-continuing explosion which tossed men and ideas about like matchsticks, crumbling traditions and institutions to dust. It is not easy to comprehend such phenomena.

There is another major problem. Inevitably, the upheaval, so crucial for Russia, so crammed with bitterness and bloodshed and change in the years that followed, so significant for subsequent events in the rest of the world, provoked a flood of writings. Gigantic piles of documents, eyewitness accounts, polemics, histories, and reports have accumulated, most of which have some usefulness, very few of which are reliable and unbiased. Somewhere in the multitude of books and articles lies the truth about the revolution. But here we face a dilemma. Painstaking, scholarly investigation has only just begun. The slow, tedious culling of fact from fiction that is essential to the forming of reliable generalizations has still to be carried out. Accomplishment of this work requires scholars with profound knowledge of Russia's history, her ideologies, institutions, and people. From such scholars must come long lists of monographs dealing exhaustively with specialized and narrow topics until we know more of the facts about the revolution. Only upon the foundation of such detailed studies can other scholars tie the events together into sound hypotheses. First the patient researchers who examine every salient problem; then powerful creative minds, like those which have worked on the French Revolution, to pull out the great explanations: until this process is completed we seek to understand without being able to learn enough to understand. Our hypotheses remain guesses. We cannot explain but must be satisfied with suggesting relationships and theories which may or may not be true.

Given this unsatisfactory state of our knowledge and desiring to understand better one of the most complex social and political upheavals of modern times, one must follow a careful plan of study. True, there are many interpretations of the events of 1917, and none of these can legitimately claim to be the exhaustive and final summation. Nonetheless, judgments can be made, for some materials are demonstrably more valuable than others. It is the first aim of this book to provide an acquaintance with those interpretations which are most rational and perceptive or which have been most favorably considered by thoughtful, well-informed men.

If the reader is to evaluate and relate the differing interpretations intelligently, he must possess considerable detailed information about the events of 1917. He must comprehend the awesome political and moral passions which then raged through Russia and which continue to influence even the most objective scholars today. It is the second purpose of this book to present information that will aid this process of evaluation.

There is also a need for a useful conceptual approach to the study of the revolution. Can an effective analysis of these complex events be made in simple terms? Or is the very truth itself embedded in the chaos and intricacy of revolutionary events, in the innumerable actions and interactions of men and ideas with the realities of an exhausted and disintegrating social order? Most significant historical processes defy simple explanations; their causes, manifestations, and consequences seem to repel neat classification. Comprehension of such events is usually best gained by studying them from many sides and from many levels. The student must examine the history, the institutions, the ideas, the characters of the men involved; he must even seek to make himself sensitive to the almost intangible tenor of a whole social climate. Somewhere in his study of the matrix of forces and events, he will begin to perceive relationships between one event and another which may be formulated as tentative hypotheses to be tested by further examination of the evidence. From this process comes knowledge. The third purpose of this book, therefore, is to provide materials which make possible a many-sided examination of the revolution, so that each reader may form his own hypotheses and begin the process of testing them.

In order to catch hold of the subject and build a conceptual framework that can guide us through the maze of detail, it is helpful to ask several specific questions about the revolution, even though they cannot be finally answered. All students of the Russian Revolution agree that some events and processes in 1917 were more significant than others. It is, for example, much more necessary to examine the impact of the First World War upon Russia than to study the operation of the Russian secondary school system in 1917. The questions posed in this book, therefore, focus upon the significant areas, and the partial answers given by different authorities are

offered because they provide meaningful insights into those events which appear to have had predominant influence.

The first specific questions pertain to the February/March Revolution: "What caused it? Who led it?" Three scholars discuss the first question. Of these, Paul Milyukov was a liberal leader during the last years of the Imperial regime and one of Russia's greatest historical scholars; Sir Bernard Pares was one of Great Britain's most learned Russian scholars; and Peter Lyashchenko is a Marxist economic historian and Soviet citizen. It is significant that these three differ not so much in the rejection of one another's views as in their emphases upon the influence of different factors.

In the selections which offer an answer to the second question of this section (Who led it?), William Henry Chamberlin seeks to establish the complete lack of any organized leadership. Leon Trotsky virulently attacks this point of view by systematically attacking *all* its adherents; then Trotsky boldly argues that the leaders of the revolution were the workers of Petrograd who had been strongly indoctrinated by the Bolshevik party. In all, the five selections of this first section fill out a dramatic picture of the era just prior to 1917 and describe the beginning of the February/March Revolution.

The second major question asks why, in the months following March, Russia hurtled at an ever-increasing pace toward more radical solutions of its problems and toward ultimate rejection of the achievements made in February/March. The continuing breakdown of political and social institutions and the growth of more extreme attitudes, on the Right as well as the Left, were the consequences of many distinct but related factors. Here it becomes clear that what is habitually referred to as *The Revolution* was in reality several revolutions, and that each of these more or less followed its own course and moved at its own speed, although there were many points of contact and interaction. Thus there was a revolution of urban workers and idle soldiers, a political revolution in the capital cities, an agrarian revolution, and revolutions developed by the strong national minorities previously held in subjection by Tsarist authority. Still another kind of political revolutionary movement was patiently organized and nurtured by Lenin and his Bolshevik party. These developing revolutions were accompanied by counter-movements, as well as worsening military and economic conditions, which heightened the tensions and hurried the rush toward what Alexander Kerensky calls the "catastrophe" of October. The six selections in this section trace the courses followed by the several clearly definable revolutions and offer evidence concerning their most important interrelationships.

The third main section, by asking the questions: "Why did the Provisional Government fall?" and "Why did the Bolsheviks successfully seize power?" raises controversial problems of the greatest importance, on which as yet there is little agreement. The four selections dealing with these questions include carefully considered judgments by outstanding representatives of the principal interpretations. The first article, by Alexander Kerensky, who was in 1917 the principal figure in the series of coalition governments roughly defined as the Provisional Government, argues that the Provisional Government was betrayed by the Moderates and Rightists, who should have supported it. Leonid Strakhovsky, an avowed Monarchist and defender of the military honor of Russia's generals, sets forth other evidence which asserts that Kerensky himself betrayed the Provisional Government and thus made its downfall inevitable. The brilliant American political scientist, Merle Fainsod, outlines the theory most widely accepted in America today, that the Bolsheviks won because they were the only well-organized, disciplined, and intelligently led political group on the scene. And the final account — from the official explanation of the Russian Communist party — holds that Marxist-Leninist political philosophy guided the Bolsheviks to victory and made such victory (given Lenin's leadership) inevitable. Clearly, the diversity of views could not be more wide. It is for the reader to study and compare and decide for himself where the truth lies, insofar as final decision is possible.

Besides offering answers to our questions, most of the excerpts in this book contain various additional attributes of value for the reader who is attempting to form valid judgments about the revolution. Several of them, while being the considered opinions of scholarly authorities, are also valuable original sources, offering deep insights into the general climate of opinion which characterized certain social groups during the revolution. Thus, for example, Paul Milyukov was a distinguished historical scholar with an unmatched knowledge of Russia's history, but he was much more. As leader of the Constitutional Democratic party* from 1905 through 1917, he played an important and active role in Russian political developments. In 1917 he served as Minister of Foreign Affairs in the first Provisional Government, and even after he left that office in May he continued to exert a powerful influence upon Russian politics. Milyukov represents that current of Western constitutional thought popular among professional and middle-class groups which dreamed of transforming Russia into a genuine constitutional state. Chained to his belief in the necessity of evolutionary development toward self-government, loyal to the middle classes, and virtually incapable of comprehending or sympathizing with the angry demands of the uncultured urban masses, Milyukov and his kind were irrevocably out of step with the revolution. Their dreams were doomed. Milyukov's analysis of the roots of the revolution tells much not only about himself but also about those social elements he represented. In other articles in this book, other men who were Milyukov's opponents during 1917 and

* Usually referred to as the Kadet (Cadet) party from its Russian initials "ka" and "de."

after give their hostile judgments of his character. Some part of the truth about the revolution is to be found in the accurate understanding of this man, the role he played, and the reactions of others to his deeds and ideas.

The work of Leon Trotsky, represented here by an excerpt from his *History of the Russian Revolution,* is another valuable source. It is the work of a man who was simultaneously a scholar of tremendous intellectual power, one of the world's great polemicists, and a leader of the Bolshevik party. Trotsky's analysis of the facts penetrates to the deepest social and historical roots; sometimes with no more than a glance he sees far more deeply than the best of our professional scholars. Yet, every word and every line of his thought is saturated with his profound faith in the Marxist doctrine and with the amazing intellectual arrogance which persuaded him that only he, Lenin, and their adherents could understand history accurately. To read Trotsky is to see how the mind of one of the greatest of the Bolshevik leaders functioned. It is an impressive experience.

In the third section, Alexander Kerensky, so long and so bitterly maligned by all sides, speaks for himself. He has brooded over the events of 1917 through all the years of his life outside of Russia. In recent years he has joined with the young American professor, Robert Browder, to examine the records of the Provisional Government with the purpose of summing up objectively the history of that institution. But in the article presented here, Kerensky develops an argument often reiterated in his books and articles. He speaks with the tortured pride of a man who is accused of the most heinous of modern crimes — betrayal of his country — and who believes that on the contrary *he was betrayed*. His argument, repeated desperately, almost hopelessly, and long rejected by many, is today being reconsidered more sympathetically. It would surely be a major shortcoming if this book deprived the reader of the opportunity to judge the character of the man who lost.

The last excerpt of the book, from *History of the Communist Party of the Soviet Union,* possesses its own special significance as an expression of the official Soviet view. This is communist propaganda, of course, stated with a simple and somewhat awkward sincerity. In this interpretation, the Bolsheviks are said to have won the revolution because they were guided by the only theory of historical change that is scientifically right, and because Lenin knew how to make the best use of this theory's precepts for his party. Within eight years after its publication 31,000,000 copies of this book had been distributed in many languages. Its interpretation has been read and apparently accepted by millions of people and thus cannot be shrugged off lightly. Moreover, because it was issued under the sponsorship of the Communist Party of the Soviet Union the reader may feel certain that it transmits some of the original Bolshevik fervor that carried the party to victory in 1917.

Implicit in all the materials included and in the questions we have asked about the revolution are many issues of immense significance for the present day. For example, there is reason to believe that Russian democracy may have failed because its defenders were too much dedicated to constitutional procedures and moderation. Does this mean that other democratic societies may be destroyed by their belief in constitutional government and doomed by their moderation? On the other hand, the evidence appears to indicate that the Bolsheviks won because of their superior political organization and their ruthless and uncompromising determination to gain power at any cost. Must political success in the 20th century invariably go to the political group that stops at nothing? Is the Soviet Union inescapably chained to the harsh policies of its Bolshevik founders? The belief of Marxist-Leninist followers that they have new and superior ways to achieve age-old human goals challenges the older theories and methods of the Western world. What will be the outcome of this competition? These questions, of course, underline only a few of the most obvious points about the impact of the revolution upon our world. Its continuing influence is visible on every hand.

A NOTE ON TECHNICALITIES

Through 1917 Russia employed the old Julian calendar, which in this century is thirteen days behind our own. Because some of the authors presented here use the Old Style dates and others the New, I have included a chronology of principal events, giving their dates in both Old and New Styles. Also because different writers use different methods of transliterating Russian words into English, and because these different methods are sometimes hotly defended by their adherents, I have not ventured to revise my authors. It seems necessary, however, to advise the reader that Miliukov, Milyukov, and Miljukov are not three different men but only one whose name has been variously transliterated. For similar reasons I have not attempted to "correct" the spelling in those selections which were first published in England.

CHRONOLOGY, 1917

Old Style	New Style	
February 22–March 2	March 7–15	The February/March Revolution
February 27	March 12	Formation of the Duma Committee and the Petrograd Soviet
March 2	March 15	Abdication of Nicholas II and formation of first Provisional Government
April 3	April 16	Lenin arrives in Petrograd
May 2	May 15	Milyukov's resignation as Minister of Foreign Affairs
May 5	May 18	Organization of First Coalition Government
June 18	July 1	The Kerensky Offensive
July 3–5	July 16–18	The July Days: unsuccessful Bolshevik demonstrations
July 24	August 6	Kerensky becomes Prime Minister in Second Coalition Government
August 25–30	September 7–12	The Kornilov revolt
September 1	September 14	Kerensky establishes the Directorate of five
September 23	October 6	Trotsky becomes president of Petrograd Soviet
September 25	October 8	Formation of Third Coalition Government
October 10	October 23	Bolsheviks decide on uprising to overthrow Provisional Government
October 12	October 25	Military Revolutionary Committee of the Soviet placed under Trotsky's direction
October 25	November 7	*Seizure of power in Petrograd*
October 26	November 8	Organization of the Bolshevik government

The Conflict of Opinion

THE MARCH REVOLUTION

"He who would write the philosophy of the Russian Revolution must of course seek its roots deep in the past, in the history of the Russian culture. Despite all the ultra-modern content of the programs, labels and slogans issued in this revolution, the reality of the Russian Revolution has revealed its intimate and indissoluble connection with all the Russian past."

— P. N. Milyukov

"While the Empress's letters wipe clean away all the scandalous charges made against her personal character . . . they also prove that she and, through her, Rasputin were the prime authors of the collapse of the Empire and of Russia."

— Sir Bernard Pares

"The war was, in Lenin's expression, 'a mighty accelerator' of the process of revolutionization . . ."

— Peter Lyashchenko

"The collapse of the Romanov autocracy in March 1917 was one of the most leaderless, spontaneous, anonymous revolutions of all time. While almost every thoughtful observer in Russia in the winter of 1916–1917 foresaw the likelihood of the crash of the existing regime no one, even among the revolutionary leaders, realized that the strikes and bread riots which broke out in Petrograd on March 8 would culminate in the mutiny of the garrison and the overthrow of the government four days later."

— William H. Chamberlin

"To the question, Who led the February revolution? we can . . . answer definitely enough: Conscious and tempered workers educated for the most part by the party of Lenin. But we must here immediately add: This leadership proved sufficient to guarantee the victory of the insurrection, but it was not adequate to transfer immediately into the hands of the proletarian vanguard the leadership of the revolution."

— Leon Trotsky

FROM MARCH TO OCTOBER

"In a word, in the labor, peasant, and nationalities questions the . . . [Provisional] Government exposed its complete creative nullity. It solved none of them, but tangled still further the Gordian knots bequeathed by the old regime. It made its final slip in . . . foreign and military policy."

— Victor Chernov

". . . from the beginning of the Revolution a desire to end the War, along with the political, economic, and social stimuli at work in every revolution, spread rapidly in both the army and the people."

— N. N. Golovine

"What is plain, and relevant to our subject, is that it was a double revolution — a peasant revolution and a political one . . ."

— David Mitrany

xv

"[Chernov's] declaration that 'the peasantry itself was the real autocrat of Russia' . . . was a statement the truth of which was never more evident than in the succeeding October, when he himself was hurled from power by those who utilised the forces that had placed his party in office."

— L. A. OWEN

"The outbreak of the Russian Revolution had, as its initial consequence, the abolition of the tsarist regime and, as its ultimate result, the complete break-down of all forms of organized life throughout Russia. One of the aspects of this breakdown was the disintegration of the Empire and the worsening of relations between its various ethnic groups. In less than a year after the Tsar had abdicated, the national question had become an outstanding issue in Russian politics."

— RICHARD PIPES

"The Bolsheviks were becoming the masters in the working-class suburbs of Petersburg. . . . The Bolsheviks met the new coalition with grim hostility; but in opposing it they displayed a tactical imagination and subtlety which could not fail to yield massive and quick rewards."

— ISAAC DEUTSCHER

THE BOLSHEVIK VICTORY

"Only by way of conspiracy, only by way of a treacherous armed struggle was it possible to break up the Provisional Government and stop the establish-ment of a democratic system in Russia after the Revolution."

— ALEXANDER KERENSKY

". . . let the facts in this case speak out the truth, and let history pronounce its verdict of guilty in betraying Russia against the former Prime Minister of the Provisional Government, to whom the dubious gains of the March Revolution were dearer than the welfare, the future, and the very existence of his country and its people."

—LEONID STRAKHOVSKY

"The enemies of Bolshevism were numerous, but they were also weak, poorly organized, divided, and apathetic. The strategy of Lenin was calculated to emphasize their divisions, neutralize their opposition, and capitalize on their apathy. In 1902 in *What Is to Be Done?* Lenin had written, 'Give us an organization of revolutionaries, and we shall overturn the whole of Russia!' On November 7, 1917, the wish was fulfilled and the deed accomplished."

— MERLE FAINSOD

"The Bolshevik Party could not have won in October 1917 if its foremost men had not mastered the theory of Marxism, if they had not learned to regard this theory as a guide to action, if they had not learned to advance the Marxist theory by enriching it with the new experience of the class struggle of the proletariat."

— *History of the Communist Party of the Soviet Union*

THE MARCH REVOLUTION:
WHAT CAUSED IT? AND WHO LED IT?

Russia's History and Culture

PAUL N. MILYUKOV

During his life in Russia Paul Milyukov gained distinction as author and historian, and because he was also an ardent defender of "Western" ideas and institutions, he was drawn into the political arena. As leader of the Constitutional Democratic party (the Cadets) he fought long and hard to transform the imperial order into a constitutional state. After the Bolshevik victory Milyukov emigrated to Western Europe where he continued both his political and scholarly activities. His principal books, concerned with Russia's intellectual and cultural history, won him acclaim as one of Russia's great historians. In the selection that follows, writing as objectively as he could at a time when he was still very close to the revolutionary events, he emphasizes the revolution's deep historical roots.

WITH what should the history of the second revolution begin? He who would write the philosophy of the Russian Revolution must of course seek its roots deep in the past, in the history of the Russian culture. Despite all the ultra-modern content of the programs, labels and slogans issued in this revolution, the reality of the Russian Revolution has revealed its intimate and indissoluble connection with all the Russian past. Just as a powerful geological cataclysm playfully casts down the crust of the latest cultural strata and brings to the surface long-hidden strata recalling the dim past — the ancient epochs of the earth's history — so the Russian Revolution laid bare for us all our historical structure, only thinly hidden by the superficial layers of recent cultural acquisitions. The study of Russian history in our day gains a singular new interest, because through the social and cultural strata displayed on the surface of the Russian upheaval the attentive observer can graphically trace the history of our past. What strikes the foreign observer of contemporary affairs, what is for him the first key to the eternal sphinxlike silence of the Russian people, has long been known to the sociologist and student of Russia's historical evolution. For the latter, Lenin and Trotsky lead movements far closer to Bolotnikov, Razin, and Pugachov — to the 17th and 18th centuries of our history — than to the latest words of European anarchic-syndicalism.[1]

In reality the fundamental trait manifested by our revolutionary process, which also constitutes the basic cause of its unfortunate result, is the weakness of the Russian State and the predominance in the

[1] Bolotnikov, Razin, and Pugachov were leaders of peasant and Cossack movements against the Tsarist regime in the 17th and 18th centuries. [Editor's note]

From P. N. Milyukov, *Istoriya Vtoroy Russkoy Revolyutsii* [History of the Second Russian Revolution], (Sofia, 1921), pp. 11–22. By permission of Boris Elkin. Translated by the editor.

country of stateless and anarchical elements. Is it not possible that this trait is the inevitable consequence of the historical process in which what continuously came from outside the state, under Rurik, under Peter the Great, and under our imperialism of the 19th and 20th centuries — outran the organic growth of the state? And another characteristic trait is the weakness of the upper social levels, so easily yielding place, and later even thrown aside by the national current. Can it be that this weakness does not flow from the whole history of our "most preeminent classes," created by the ruler for state needs in the manner practised in the autocracies of the East, and preserving up to the very last moment the character of the old "service" nobility? Is it possible that the traditional view of the Russian peasant about the land, the memory of its historical destiny preserved in the very name "pomeshchich'ey," is not tied with the past while coming into the present?[2] And the almost complete absence of a "bourgeoisie" in the true sense of the word? Its political impotence, with the whole wide application of the revolutionary sobriquet "bourgeois" to all who wear starched collars and derbies? Doesn't this remind us of the profound differences between us and the European West in the history of the whole struggle for political freedom, of the vast chronological distance between the beginning of this struggle there and here, and the unavoidable consequences of this distance: the confluence with us of political and social revolution, and in the social upheaval — the confusion of a struggle against the precariously organized and swiftly destroyed serfdom with a struggle against a completely unformed "capitalism"? Read the history of the French Revolution of Taine — and you will see how all that which applied to the "nobility" in the civil war of the great [French] revolution was repeated down to the last detail in our revolution by the

slogan "bourgeoisie." We changed, of course, only the slogan; the issues of the civil war remained the same. Yes, and how could it have been otherwise when both the development of Russian industry and the development of towns were to a considerable degree the fruit of the last decades, and when even 30 years ago earnest writers thoughtfully considered the question whether Russia might in general escape "the stage of capitalism"?

Closely connected with the two characteristics mentioned, the weakness of the Russian State and the primitiveness of the Russian social structure, is a third characteristic trait of our revolutionary process: the ideological helplessness and utopian aspirations — the "maximalism" — of the Russian intelligentsia. Once I defended this intelligentsia against P. B. Struve and his "Signposts";[3] but I defended it only in one sense: I defended its right not to seek roots in our past, where, as has already been said, lie only the roots of our languor and weakness. Its backwardness is the unavoidable consequence of the shallowness of our cultural development. How could this be otherwise when all of our new cultural tradition (since Peter) has been wholly created by only *eight generations* of our predecessors, and when this work was sharply and irrevocably isolated from the indigenous culture of a long period of national unconsciousness: a period which in other cultured nations forms the prehistoric epoch? Standing on the shoulders of only eight generations in all, we were able to absorb the cultural acquisitions of the West — and we assimilated them with a supple and delicate sensibility which astonishes foreigners. We enriched these borrowings with our own national traits, which struck the foreigners as a strange grafting of refinement to the primitive. But we could not do one thing: we were unable to develop anything like a

---

[2] *Pomeshchich'ey* — land belonging to the landlord, a reminder of the serfdom which existed in Russia until 1861. [Editor's note]

[3] *Signposts: A Collection of Essays concerning the Russian Intelligentsia*, Moscow, 1909. This was a collective work by several authors, including Struve, which denounced the defects of the Russian intelligentsia. [Editor's note]

firm Western cultural type. This Western cultural stability we still tend to call "narrowness," and we continue to prefer that infinite freedom of the Slav nature, "the most free in the world," about which the brilliant observer Herzen spoke with neither tenderness nor sorrow. In my other works I have described how Western idealism in its most extreme and personal manifestations was easily implanted in the soil of this incomplete cultural type, and how as a consequence, serious political thought developed slowly. I have also tried to trace how successes were made in the direction of mutual agreement and gradual liberation (on the one side from utopian and on the other from class elements) of the two chief currents of our social thought: the socialistic current and the liberal current at the time of their first collisions with life. It seemed to me (in 1904) that the further development of the political struggle would bring the elimination of a whole series of differences of opinion which passed as principles, and would establish the possibility of joint action by both currents in the struggle with the common enemy, the old régime. The one and a half decades which have passed since that time have shown me that I appraised the possibility of this rapprochement too optimistically. Since then the presently acting political parties were formed, and instead of cooperation an irreconcilable mutual struggle began. In the process of this struggle many of the utopias which I had thought buried were resurrected; and the political circles which, according to my conjectures, should have struggled against these utopias proved to be intellectually compatible with them and incapable of staunch opposition. Because of this incomplete adjustment of Russian political parties to the conditions and demands of Russian reality, Russia has paid with the failure of two of its revolutions and a fruitless dissipation of national resources so dear in a country with such poor resources.

Of course, the imperfection and immaturity of political ideas in a milieu of statelessness and weak social strata cannot be presented as the sole explanation of the misfortunes which have overtaken our political movement up to this time. Another factor is the unconsciousness and darkness of the Russian popular masses, which, in truth, made utopian the application to our realities even of such ideas as were completely opportune and already partly realized among peoples more prepared for direct participation in political activity. The popular masses — "the soul of the people" — themselves became the object of the intelligentsia's utopias in the past — and have hardly ceased being so at the present time. Personally I have always been far from those who were prepared to exalt the Russian people as a chosen people, "a people bearing God in its heart," and from those who by kneeling before it, debase in every way the Russian intelligentsia and the new Russian cultural traditions. In the struggle with these tendencies in their various manifestations, I employed considerable efforts during the first half of my public activities, when these tendencies advanced vigorously and seemed more dangerous than now. But I am also far from those, who under the influence of the frightful trials and grievous experiences suffered during recent months, now tend to speak about the "brute-mob." Yes, of course, the people preserved the world view of other centuries than ours, but in the last years of the old regime it was deliberately held in darkness and ignorance by the adherents of this regime. This people actually stood before the observers of its psychology almost as if it were some other lower race. On the basis of this cultural difference it was easy for international socialism to make a deep social rift and to fan into blazing flame the social hostility of the people to the "Varangians," the "zemshchiny," and the "druzhiny," expressing themselves in Slavophilic terms.[4] But

4 The Scandinavian adventurers who are generally believed to have established the first Russian state were called *Varangians*. A Varangian Prince or leader was customarily supported by a group of

the elements of truly healthy international-ism found themselves not beneath but above — in the cultural strata, in ideas, and institutions. And the growth of interna-tional culture has been halted by the de-struction of these upper levels — we cannot say for how long. However that may be, the correction of the consequences of our history and the errors of the revolution goes in the same direction as before: in the direc-tion of the reestablishment of our cultured strata so mercilessly destroyed by the revo-lution. In this sense all the democratic pro-grams, which, although they have not yet given anything to the people, desire to do "everything through the people," must be reviewed. The groundless disillusionment with the people after the just as groundless bowing before them must not of course return us to that system "of distrust of the people, restrained by fear," which, accord-ing to the pointed definition of Gladstone, lies at the basis of reactionary politics. The essence of correct policy, adapted to the actual level of the masses, must, making use of Gladstone's expression, consist in "trust in the people, limited by common sense." This formula, of course, is not compatible with the formula of complete and unlimited sovereignty of the people. It is necessary clearly to understand this, to tell oneself this definitely, and to draw from it the necessary political conclusions. In politics absolute recipes suitable for all times and for all cir-cumstances do not exist. It is time to under-stand that even *democratic* policies do not constitute an exception to this principle. It is time for us to master the idea that even in democracy's slogans there is no panacea or drug for all illnesses.

There is still another reservation within the boundaries of this question about the

masses as a political factor. There are people who would be prepared to seek in the char-acter of these masses not only those chang-ing traits in which the course of our histori-cal evolution has been imprinted, but also that immutable mystical core which the German metaphysicians, as well as the new-est sociologist of the type of Gustave Le-bon, have called "the soul of the people," *l'âme ancestrale*. Examining the French psychology of wartime, Lebon sought in this "ancestral spirit" an explanation for why a recently "decadent" France was sud-denly transformed in the face of the enemy into an heroic France. Alas! The course and issue of the Russian Revolution up to the present does not empower us to seek similar parallels. The traditional compari-son of 1613 and 1813, it is true, recalls the moments of lucid national consciousness and the extraordinary popular efforts of which the Russian people have been capa-ble when they became conscious that dan-ger threatened their very existence.[5] Per-haps one may hope that in 1919 such an awakening in the face of a great national catastrophe will take a more cultured form — something like the German renascence at the beginning of the 19th century. Perhaps this catastrophe will serve as the shock which will end the prehistoric, subcon-scious, practically ethnographic existence of the people, and will begin an historical period of coherent self-awareness and un-broken social memory. We would in this event, after a very great delay, go along the road already long since passed over by cultured peoples. But in waiting until all these hopes are realized, we must acknowl-edge that the very hopes of this generation serve, in a way, as chronological landmarks. Our Russian *âme ancestrale* obviously con-tinues to represent that plasma on which

---

warriors called a *druzhina*. In imperial political theory the tsars and many of their nobles were descendants of these Varangians. By emphasizing these names in their propaganda the enemies of the imperial system magnified the "foreignness" of its origins and institutions. *Zemshchina,* a word whose significance is drawn from the reign of Ivan the Terrible (1533–1584), as used here connotes a nation belonging not to the people and their Tsar but to the nobles. [Editor's note]

[5] The Time of Troubles, an era of dynastic failure, civil wars, and social anarchy, was ended in 1613 by what Milyukov apparently considered a "na-tional awakening." Another "national awaken-ing" presumably accompanied Napoleon's inva-sion of and flight from Russia in 1812 and Russia's invasion of Western Europe in 1813. [Editor's note]

the marks of history have been imprinted only weakly and fragmentarily. Its basic virtues remain that universal adaptability and plasticity in which Dostoevsky recognized the fundamental virtue of the Russian spirit—idealizing it as "Pan-humanity." In its political application, the formlessness of this spirit is manifested as that natural, pre-state "anarchism," that "natural condition of man," described in the old political doctrines, which "the great writer of the Russian land" so glowingly and so powerfully expressed, reflecting as in a mirror this condition of the popular spirit to the surprise of the civilized world.

We repeat, the philosopher of the history of the Russian Revolution will not be able to evade all of these deep roots and threads tying the second Russian Revolution with the whole course and the result of the Russian historical process. . . .

Let us consider the immense influence of a factor not mentioned before, but possessing *negative* significance of the highest importance. If the general character of the Russian Revolution was determined in significant degree by our past, then its character precisely as a revolution, as a violent upheaval, was determined by the effectiveness of a factor which opposed the peaceful resolution of the conflicts and internal contradictions between the old *forms* of political life and the lack of room for *content* in those forms. *The instinct of self-preservation of the old regime and its defenders:* such was the negative factor.

In the work of 1903–1904 mentioned above, I explained in detail how this instinct of self-preservation inevitably led to a policy of continuously heightening repressions and to the division of Russia into two camps: official Russia, and all the rest of Russia in which the cultured and popular elements alike were irreconcilably inclined in relation to the pre-reform political policies. Not only in these years, but even far earlier, in the 60's and the 40's [of the 19th century], and at the end of the 18th century, it was obvious that conflict of the old state order with the new demands was only

a matter of time. The whole world view of the Russian intelligentsia for at least the last six generations was formed beneath the embers of this coming conflict. It is not strange that this world view came forth so one-sided. To describe all the history of this conflict would mean, essentially, to retell all the history of Russian culture for the last two centuries. Naturally this task cannot be the purpose of the present account. It is enough for me to refer to my earlier works already mentioned, which, by anticipating the coming conflict, prepared Russian and foreign public opinion for it to the best of my abilities.

Perhaps it would be useful here to stop only on the last stage of this conflict between the old state order and the new social order—in that last decade when the chronic conflict passed over to the stage of *insincere concessions* by the government to the public currents. This decade is marked by the open beginning of political life in Russia under the aegis of the first popular political representative body.[6] German publicists have already invented for this period the term, very much to the point: the epoch of "pseudo-constitutionalism" (Scheinkonstitutionalismus). If it is possible to formulate in one word the reason why, with the first government concessions, the conflict was not stopped, but assumed a drawn-out character which ultimately led to the present catastrophe,—then the explanation is given in this word: Scheinkonstitutionalismus. The concessions of the government could not satisfy educated society and the people, and not just because they were inadequate and incomplete. They were insincere and false, and in giving them the government did not for one minute regard them as concessions made once and for all. I recall the moment when Count Witte, in November, 1905, after the October Manifesto, invited me for a political discussion.[7]

[6] The elected State Duma. [Editor's note]

[7] Count Sergius Witte, one of Russia's most intelligent officials and Minister of Finance until his dismissal in 1903, was brought back into service in 1905 to negotiate the Treaty of Portsmouth, which

I told him that no public cooperation with the government was possible as long as the government would not openly pronounce the word: *Constitution*. Let a constitution be issued, I said, but it was essential that it be given definitively. Count Witte did not conceal from me that he could not carry out this condition, because "the Tsar did not desire" it. It is well known that Emperor Nicholas considered that even the Manifesto of October 17 was given "in a fever," and he was never reconciled even with its more than modest concessions. Of course, neither did Count Witte want a constitution, owing to his old Slavophil views; even such a public figure as Dmitry Nikolayevich Shipov did not want a constitution.[8] For the defense of the ambiguity thus created, a special party was formed, the "Union of October 17," and the whole following decade was passed under the sign of political hypocrisy.[9] Since the country could not be satisfied with this, the very existence of representative institutions served only to widen the base of the further struggle between the public and the defenders of the old order. If the opposition of the State Duma served as the bulwark for the public in this situation, not falling silent even in the most difficult moments of this institution's existence, then the State Council served as the bulwark of the government, taking to itself all the strength and concentrating all the zeal of the bureaucrats of the old regime. As a result of the struggles of these two centers, for ten years there was practically no legislation at all in Russia. All projects of reform, even the most moderate, were bottled up under the "cork" of the State Council, which was trans-

formed through the years into the true graveyard of the State Duma's good efforts. Only those measures which the government in alliance with the governing classes desired were passed through the legislative institutions. Thus the agrarian reform of Stolypin was passed; thus were passed the laws about Finland, shameful for the Russian name. But the suppleness and complaisance of the Octobrists soon seemed inadequate to the government. The course of policy turned always more to the right. "Constitutionalism" became always more unreal, and the order of the day became a most shameless "nationalism." The old formula of Uvarov, "Orthodoxy, Autocracy, and Nationality," was exhumed from the archives, slightly renovated, and put forth seriously as a platform for elections and as a regular political program.[10] The desire of Emperor Nicholas II — to preserve autocracy just as it was "in olden times" — was accepted not alone by the "Union of the Russian People," which had called forth this declaration of the Tsar; it was also put into practice by political figures, who gave themselves out to be statesmen and further, and more candidly, proposed themselves one against another as organizers of changes of government. There is no need here to mention names. The names are remembered by all; many of the persons bearing them paid with tragic deaths for their guilt before the motherland and before the Russian people. This — *their* work, coupled with all the heightened influence of favorites and rogues at the court, created in the country that state of almost complete uncertainty in the future which, properly speaking, prepared the psychology of revolution by isolating the court and government from all levels of the population and from all the nationalities of the Russian State.

For the wisest of these servitors of the old

---

ended the Russo-Japanese War. After this success Witte was able to persuade the Emperor to issue the Manifesto of October 17, a series of concessions and reforms which helped to end the 1905 Revolution and which could have served as a springboard to a genuine constitutional regime. [Editor's note]

[8] D. N. Shipov: a well-known moderate liberal, who favored local self-government but opposed the constitutionalists. [Editor's note]

[9] Members of the "Union of October 17" were called "Octobrists." [Editor's note]

[10] Count S. S. Uvarov, Minister of Education in the first half of the nineteenth century, formulated this slogan which excellently summed up the philosophy of the reactionary Emperor Nicholas I (1825–1855). [Editor's note]

regime it was clear that with such a tense public mood, with such an unstable equilibrium maintained with difficulty by a policy of repressions and based upon an artificially organized, insignificant minority, Russia could not withstand any serious external shock or internal blow. The experience of 1905, it would seem, should have served as a lesson. At that time the consequences of the unfortunate war were liquidated with great difficulty and the government was saved from the inevitable results: internal revolution. Count Witte was summoned especially to carry out this mission. The blunders of the first Russian Revolution [1905] and the support of Europe made it possible for him to execute it brilliantly. But the short-sighted government distrusted its best and most faithful defender. Count Witte barely secured for himself the right to save this government, and remained at his post only until the conclusion of the loan in France and until the return of the Russian Army from Manchuria. His services were not needed further. His rivals recommended the liquidation of the concessions made "in fever" — concessions for which they could never forgive Count Witte. And the struggle against the young popular representative body was begun, which led to the first violation of the "pseudo-constitution," to the publication of the electoral law of June 3, 1906. This [law] conclusively isolated the government from the population and transferred the popular representative body to the hands of favorites and favored parties. Knocked together pell-mell, the state cart barely creaked along up to the first shock.

Was it possible to prevent [that shock]? The adherents of the old regime considered that it was both possible and necessary — in alliance with Germany. But life carried Russian policy in another direction, to the side of the states of the "Alliance," and the newly-born Russian representative assembly played here a celebrated role. One way or another, with the division of Europe into two camps, Russia could not fail to be drawn into the international conflict. She could only avoid the guilt of creating conflicts, but for this her Balkan policy was insufficiently wise and clear-sighted. The general unintelligence of the government led to a situation in which, moving more or less consciously toward a possible conflict, Russia proved to be unprepared for it in the military sense. In external policy as also in the question about the strengthening of military power, the State Duma had a certain influence — and by this means tied itself with the patriotically inclined political circles. In this way it first acquired a certain independence from the pressures of the highest "circles" and prepared for a role as a serious political factor in the event of an external conflict — becoming more serious as the government proved itself to be more weak, confused, and unprepared. In this situation the role of intellectual leader of the nation inevitably went to the State Duma.

And here it came, this war — in the form of a vast world conflict. In the series of factors determining the *special character* of the second revolution, the first place of course belongs to the war of 1914–1918. Many, many of the phenomena which are usually considered specifically revolutionary actually preceded the revolution, and were created precisely by the circumstances of wartime.

Rasputin and the Empress Alexandra

BERNARD PARES

The English-speaking world owes much of its knowledge about Russia to the indefatigable enthusiasm, energy, and intelligence of Sir Bernard Pares (1867–1949). Besides teaching almost continuously from 1908 to 1949 at the Universities of Liverpool and London, and in the United States, he was attached to the Russian Army from 1914–1917, visited Russia many times, directed the School of Slavonic and East European Studies, and found time to write and translate numerous excellent works on Russia. In the article here excerpted, Pares describes the destructive influence of the Imperial court and its chief actors.

THE publication of the letters of the Tsaritsa to her husband for the first time showed in black and white Rasputin's enormous political significance. But those who took the trouble to wade through that mass of loose English were probably too overcome by the sweep of the vast tragedy to realize at first the unique importance of the letters as historical material. It is to this aspect of the subject that this article is devoted.

The Rasputin tragedy passed at the time behind closed doors, except for Rasputin's own entire indifference to public scandal. By now almost every one of the persons who could give valuable first-hand evidence on the subject has said his word. M. Gilliard, tutor to the Tsarevich, a man of great good sense and good feeling, has given a beautiful picture of the home life of the Imperial family, the accuracy of which has been confirmed both by the Provisional and the Soviet Governments. We have for what it is worth the Apologia of Madame Vyrubov, the only person who was with the family continually, and Rasputin's chosen go-between for his communications with the Empress. A slighter record is given by another friend of the Empress, Madame Lili Dehn. The Head

of the Police Department, Beletsky, has told a typical story of ministerial intrigue centred round Rasputin. The French Ambassador, M. Paléologue, has issued a current record of events, evidently touched up for publication, which gives the atmosphere of grand ducal and higher society, but also connects Rasputin at point after point with political events of the most critical importance. Now we have also the important record of the President of the Third and Fourth Dumas, Mr. Michael Rodzianko, prepared in exile without many materials but preserving the details of his various conversations with the Emperor, which were evidently written down with care at the time.

Rasputin, who was under fifty at the time of his death, was born in the village of Pokrovskoe on the Tura, near Tobolsk in Siberia. Like many peasants he had no surname; Rasputin, which means "dissolute," was a nickname early given him by his fellow peasants. He suddenly went off to the Verkhne-Turski Monastery near his home, where were several members of the *Khlysty*, a sect who mingled sexual orgies with religious raptures and who were emphatically condemned by the Orthodox Church. On his return he became a *stran-*

From Sir Bernard Pares, "Rasputin and the Empress: Authors of the Russian Collapse," *Foreign Affairs,* VI, No. 1 (October, 1927), pp. 140–49, 153–54. Reprinted by permission of *Foreign Affairs,* October, 1927. Copyright by the Council on Foreign Relations, Inc., New York.

nik, or roving man of God, not a monk, not in orders, but one with a self-given commission from heaven, such as have often appeared in Russian history, especially at critical times. Meanwhile, he lived so scandalous a life that his village priest investigated it with care. That he habitually did much the same things as the *Khlysty* is conclusively proved; but that he was actually one of the sect has not been definitely established. Certainly to the end of his life he alternated freely between sinning and repenting, and professed the view that great sins made possible great repentances. He seduced a large number of women, several of whom boasted of the fact, or repented and confessed it to others. The village priest reported him to Bishop Antony of Tobolsk, who made a more thorough enquiry and found evidence which he felt bound to hand over to the civil authorities. During the enquiry Rasputin disappeared. He went to St. Petersburg, and as a great penitent secured the confidence of Bishop Theophan, head of the Petersburg Religious Academy, and Confessor to the Empress, a man whose personal sanctity has been recognized by everyone. He secured also the patronage of the Grand Duchess Militsa, daughter of King Nicholas of Montenegro, a lady with a strong taste for the sensational, and also that of her future brother-in-law, the Grand Duke Nicholas. It was these who introduced him to the Palace.

The Empress Alexandra, formerly Princess Alix of Hesse Darmstadt, was a daughter of the English Princess Alice and a favorite granddaughter of Queen Victoria, from whom she may be said to have taken all the ordinary part of her mental environment. The unusual feature in her character was her strong mysticism. Her family was scourged with the haemophilic ailment; all the male children of her sister Princess Irene of Prussia suffered from it. It does not appear in females, but is transmitted by them to males. Its effect is that the slightest accident may set up internal bleeding, which there is no known way of arresting.

Children suffering from it may die at any moment, and on almost any occasion, though if they live to the age of 13 they may in some measure overcome it; Rasputin prophesied such an issue for the Tsarevich Alexis. Much of the tragedy in the position of the Empress lay in the fact that after she had given birth to four charming and healthy daughters, her only son, the long-desired heir to the throne, suffered from this scourge, and that she well knew that his disease came through herself.

In every other domestic respect the family was ideally happy. Husband and wife literally adored each other; the children were equally united with them and with each other. The Empress was the pillar of the house, their actual nurse and attendant in time of sickness. She brought them up entirely in English ideas; they had cold baths and slept on camp beds; they talked largely in English. The family as a whole, in its clean-minded life, represented a veritable oasis in the corruption which was so prevalent in higher Russian society, and we may imagine that with that world this aspect of their isolation was one of their chief offenses. They lived almost as much apart from it as if they were settlers in Canada.

The Empress's nature was singularly narrow and obstinate; Rodzianko rightly describes her as "essentially a creature of will." She had a fondness for her first "little home" at Hesse Darmstadt, but a strong antipathy for the Emperor William; indeed the Prussian monarchy found many of its bitterest critics among the smaller reigning German families. She regarded herself as essentially English, but she had frankly embraced the country of her adored husband, and more than that, she had embraced the Russian autocracy. She repeatedly speaks of herself as "anointed by God," and once as "Russia's mother." There is on record a conversation between her and Queen Victoria in which she put very strongly this difference between the English monarchy and the Russian. For her, Russia was the Russian people, above all the peasantry. Society she identified with the general corruption which she saw around her. She was always, we may be sure, entirely against the Duma and against the concession of a Russian constitution. Any such suggestion she regarded as a direct wrong to her son, and denounced in the strongest language.

When she married, three of her husband's last five ancestors had perished by assassination. Her first appearance before the Russian public was in the funeral procession of her father-in-law, and the reign from start to finish was soaked in an atmosphere of fatality. She had an antipathy to all Court ceremonies. The slightest accident filled her with apprehension. In the period when her most ardent desire was to give an heir to the throne, she met in France a charlatan soul doctor, Philippe, who was brought to Russia but expelled, despite her protection, for meddling in politics during the Japanese War. Philippe gave her a bell as a token that she was to scare away all other counsellors from her husband. She refers to this several times in her letters. Bishop Theophan, when he introduced Rasputin to the Court, appears only to have thought that he was substituting a Russian influence for a foreign.

Rasputin at first kept quiet and studied his ground. He saw the Imperial family infrequently, and his presence was sought only to comfort the nerves of the Empress and her husband, and to re-assure them as to the health of their son. M. Gilliard, who was nearly all day with his charge, saw him but once. The meetings ordinarily took place at the little house of Madame Vyrubov outside the Palace. Soon, however, Rasputin went on openly with his earlier scandalous life. Toward the end of 1911 sensational happenings attracted public attention to him. Among his former supporters had been the robust Bishop of Saratov, Hermogen, a very strong monarchist, and the Monk Heliodor, a notable and popular preacher, also very conservative. An attempt was made to push through the Synod an authorization to ordain Ras-

putin a priest. This was defeated in view of his well-known dissoluteness. Hermogen was one of its most vigorous opponents. Direct interference from the Court obtained at least a partial reversion of the decision of the Synod. Hermogen again was most vigorous in his protests. He and Heliodor, acting together, arranged a meeting with Rasputin which resulted in threats on both sides; Rasputin threw himself on the Bishop as if to strangle him, and when pulled off departed threatening vengeance. Hermogen was then banished to his diocese by order of the Emperor and, as he still refused to submit, both he and Heliodor were ultimately relegated to monasteries. The Emperor had acted illegally in imposing such a sentence on a bishop without trial by a church court.

This was not the end. Shortly afterwards one Novoselov, a specialist on Russian sects who lectured at the Religious Academy near Moscow, issued a pamphlet giving full details of Rasputin's seductions, which seemed to be numberless. The book was immediately suppressed, but was widely quoted by Russian newspapers beginning with "The Voice of Moscow," the organ of Guchkov. He was leader of the Duma, and for a short time its President, and he had at first hoped to play the part of tribune of the people at the palace and to carry the Emperor with him for reform. But he had been severely rebuffed, and chose this ground for attack. The papers were now forbidden to speak of Rasputin. At this time the preliminary censorship no longer existed, and such orders by the government were therefore illegal. Fines could be imposed after publication, but fines in this case the newspapers were ready to pay. Guchkov led a debate in the Duma on this infraction of the law. Rodzianko, who tried to limit and moderate the debate as much as possible, obtained an audience from the Emperor, and speaking with absolute plainness laid a number of data before him. "I entreat you," he ended, "in the name of all that is holy for you, for Russia, for the happiness of your successor, drive off from you this filthy adventurer, disperse the growing apprehensions of people loyal to the throne." "He is not here now," said the Emperor. Rodzianko took him up, "Let me tell everyone that he will not return." "No," said Nicholas, "I cannot promise you that, but I fully believe all you say. I feel your report was sincere, and I trust the Duma because I trust you." Next day he authorized Rodzianko to make a full investigation, and the plentiful material in the possession of the Synod was handed over to him. The Empress tried to get these papers back, but Rodzianko gave a stout refusal to her messenger, saying that she was as much the subject of the Emperor as himself. When he was ready with his conclusions he asked for another audience, but Nicholas put him off. He threatened to resign, and was invited to send in a report. Later he heard that it had been studied by Nicholas and the Grand Duke of Hesse, brother of the Empress, while they were together at Livadia in Crimea. The Grand Duke, as is known, in no way supported the attitude of the Empress.

For the time Rasputin disappeared. In the summer of 1912, while the Imperial family was at a hunting box in Poland, the Tsarevich fell on the gunwale of a boat; the bruise set up internal bleeding and for some weeks his life was despaired of. All the family were distracted with grief. The best doctors declared themselves impotent. The Empress then ordered a telegram to be sent to Rasputin, who replied: "This illness is not dangerous; don't let the doctors worry him." From the time of the reception of the telegram the boy rapidly recovered. There is no doubt as to these facts, which were testified to unanimously by various witnesses. Nor is there evidence of any kind for the supposition that the illness was artificially created.

Stolypin before his death in 1911 had reported in the strongest language against Rasputin. The attitude of his successor, Count Kokovtsev, was practically the same. The Empress when she met him turned her back on him, and he was curtly dismissed

from the post of Premier in January, 1914. The aged Goremykin who succeeded him, and who possessed throughout the complete confidence of the Empress, summed up the question to Rodzianko in the words, "C'est une question clinique."

When war broke out, Rasputin was lying dangerously ill at Tobolsk, where one of his female victims had tried to assassinate him. He sent a telegram to Madame Vyrubov, "Let papa (the Emperor) not plan war. It will be the end of Russia and of all of us. We shall be destroyed to the last man." The Emperor was very annoyed at this, and never was he more at one with his people than when he appeared on the balcony of the Winter Palace and the vast crowd kneeled in front of him. For the first period of the war the Empress devoted herself to hospital work, and spared herself no labor or unpleasantness in the care of the sick; on matters of administration she only ventured tentative and timid opinions.

The discovery of gross munition scandals in the early summer of 1915 roused a wave of national indignation, and seemed at first to bring Russia nearer to an effective constitution than ever before. It must be understood that the constitutional question was still unsettled. The Duma had come to stay, as even the Empress at this time admitted. In spite of a manipulated and limited franchise, it had more and more come to represent the nation. The limits on its competence, however, remained; it had once succeeded by moral pressure in removing a Minister (Timiriazev), but the Ministers were not responsible to it. As is clear from the Emperor's talks with Rodzianko, he certainly did not recognize his famous edict of October 30, 1905, which gave full legislative powers to the Duma, as the grant of a Constitution, and the Duma's rights had been whittled down since then both by limitations imposed at the outset in the fundamental laws of 1906, and also in practice ever since.

The Emperor was in entire agreement with his people as to the needs of his army. He appealed for the utmost efforts, and at

Rodzianko's request he established a War Industries Committee on which the Duma was to be represented. The Alliance itself worked in the same direction, for democratic France and England desired to see as hearty as possible a coöperation of the Russian people in the prosecution of the war. The War Minister, Sukhomlinov, who had been at least criminally negligent, was dismissed; the Emperor also got rid of those of his Ministers who were at best half-hearted about the war, Nicholas Maklakov, Shcheglovitov and Sabler, and replaced them by men who had the confidence of the country. It looked as if the movement would go a good deal further. The bulk of the Duma, containing nearly all its best brains, had practically formed into one party under the name of the Progressive Bloc, and it asked for the definite adoption of the principle that the Ministry as a whole should be such as to possess the public confidence. Those of the Ministers who were of the same view, at this time a majority in the Cabinet, went even further; they wrote a letter to the Sovereign asking that the aged and obviously incompetent Prime Minister should be changed. If things had not stopped here, Russia would have done what all her Allies were doing at the same time, namely have formed a national and patriotic Coalition Ministry; but, beyond that, she would also have completed the process towards a Constitution which, though often interrupted, had been going on since the Emancipation of the Serfs in 1861.

It was here that the Empress intervened, with the assistance and advice of Rasputin. She got the Emperor back to Tsarskoe Selo for several weeks and persuaded him to dismiss from the Chief Command the Grand Duke Nicholas, who was popular with the Duma and the country. This both she and Rasputin regarded as the most essential victory of all. She then obtained the prorogation of the Duma, and its President and the delegates of other public bodies who begged the Emperor to reverse this decision were met with the most chilling refusal. She then persuaded her husband that all the Ministers who had, so to speak, struck work against Premier Goremykin should be replaced as soon as possible. We thus enter the critical period which changed the war from being an instrument for producing a Russian Constitution into the principal cause of the Russian Revolution. From now till the final collapse Russia was governed by the Empress, with Rasputin as her real Prime Minister.

Two incidents in the summer and autumn sharpened the conflict between the Court and the public over the influence of Rasputin. In the summer Rasputin varied his dissolute orgies with a severe course of repentance and visited the tombs of the Patriarchs in Moscow. Presumably he overdid the repentance, for he followed it up with a visit to a notorious resort, the Yar, where he got drunk and behaved in the most scandalous way. His proceedings were recorded in detail by the police, who were present, and were reported by them to one of the most loyal servants of the Emperor, General Dzhunkovsky, at this time Commander of the Palace Guard. Dzhunkovsky presented the report without comment to the Emperor. Next day he was dismissed from all appointments, and the protest of another intimate friend of the Emperor, Prince Orlov, had the same result. The Empress flatly refused to believe such reports and persisted in regarding them as machinations of the police.

In 1915 the Emperor was starting with his son for the front when the Tsarevich was taken violently ill in the train, which thereupon returned to Tsarskoe Selo. Rasputin was summoned at once and from the time of his visit the boy recovered, as in 1912. Rasputin often played on this theme. Once he fell into fervent prayer and when he had ended declared that he had saved the Emperor from assassination. He made many happy guesses, some of which were almost uncanny. On the other hand, the Empress herself gives several instances, some of them conspicuous, of predictions which went all wrong.

Neither the Emperor nor the Empress had at this time any thought whatsoever of a separate peace; the Emperor, we know, never entertained such an idea even after abdication. Up till December 30, the date of the last of the Empress's letters, we know that she regarded victory in the war as a foregone conclusion, that her chief anxiety was that Russian influence might be overshadowed by British when the victorious peace was made, and that her main desire was that the victory of Russia should be entirely the triumph of her husband. Nicholas at times spoke tentatively of reforms, but throughout this period insisted that they could only follow after the war.

In going to the front the Emperor had *ipso facto* more or less abandoned the administration to his wife, who definitely describes herself as his "wall in the rear," speaks even of "wearing the trousers" in the struggle against internal enemies, recalls the time when Catherine the Great (who had much more drastically disposed of her husband) received the Ministers, and in the end is absolutely certain that she is "saving Russia." Rasputin, who had on several occasions pushed suggestions as to the war, gradually became the ultimate factor in all decisions. Practically no Minister could be appointed except on his recommendation or after accepting allegiance to him.

He initiated the period of his power by making himself absolutely supreme in all Church affairs. Let me sum up his principal achievements in this domain. He dismisses an adverse Minister of Religion, Samarin, who had been the elected Marshal of the Moscow Nobility; he dismisses his successor, Volzhin, appointed at his own desire; he practically appoints a third Minister, Raiev; he commands a public prayer-giving throughout the country, insisting that the order should not pass through the Synod; he appoints as Metropolitan of Petrograd, Pitirim, a contemptible sycophant of his own; he negatives a project of the Synod to create seven Metropolitan Sees in Russia; through one of his subordinates and in violation of all rules he creates a new Saint, St. John of Tobolsk.

But there was hardly any other department of administration with which he did not interfere. He settles at various times and in various ways the administration of the food supply; he orders an absurdly simplified way of dealing with the question of rations; he confers repeatedly with the Minister of Finance, whose resignation he at first demands and then defers, and he insists on the issue of an enormous loan. He secures that the whole passenger transport of the country should be suspended for six days for the passage of food — a measure which is made futile by the failure to collect the food supplies at the proper places for transport. He repeatedly interferes both in military appointments and in military operations; he secures the suspension of Sukhomlinov's trial; he secures the dismissal of his successor, Polivanov, who according to all military evidence, including that of Hindenburg, in his few months of office brought about a wonderful recovery of the efficiency of the Russian army; he orders an offensive; he countermands an offensive; he dictates the tactics to be followed in the Carpathians; he even demands to be informed in advance of all military operations, and to know the exact day on which they are to begin, in order that he may decide the issue by his prayers; he arranges the details of the future military entry into Constantinople. He removes the Foreign Minister, Sazonov, who in Russia was the main arch of the alliance, the trusted friend of the British and French Ambassadors. He adjourns and opposes any execution of the Emperor's promise to give autonomy to Poland. He dictates telegrams to the King of Serbia and to the King of Greece.

*   *   *

While the Empress's letters wipe clean away all the scandalous charges made against her personal character, while they show that up to Rasputin's death she was a fervent Russian patriot who had no thought of a separate peace with Germany, they also prove that she and, through her, Rasputin were the prime authors of the collapse of the Empire and of Russia.

The Bolshevist leaders were far away in Switzerland or Canada, and their not numerous followers were out of the picture. The leaders of the Duma, largely in answer to the pressure of Russia's Allies, were doing all that they could to postpone the explosion till after the War. Up to the intervention of the fatal pair in the late Summer of 1915, it seemed that the war itself was only bringing nearer what practically all Russia desired. Apart from the terrible depression that followed on the disillusionment of 1915, Russia was then confronted with a monstrous régime which would have seemed impossible in some small duchy in the Middle Ages. In the midst of a world-wide struggle, in a time of the closest collaboration with the best brains of Western statesmanship, the Russian Ministers were selected by an ignorant, blind, and hysterical woman on the test of their subservience to an ignorant, fantastic, and debauched adventurer, a test which they could only satisfy by open-eyed self-abasement or at the best by cynical passivity, and the supreme commands of the adventurer permeated every detail of government in every branch of the administration. Meanwhile, in his drunken revels he babbled publicly of his influence over the Empress, held a daily *levée* attended by the worst financial swindlers, and preached views both on the war and on the government of the country, which were shared only by the avowed friends of Germany, who evidently had easier access to him than any one else.

It was under the leadership of such a government that the lives of millions of peasants were thrown into the furnace of the World War.

Economic and Social Consequences of the War

PETER I. LYASHCHENKO

Peter I. Lyashchenko, a "legal Marxist" and a recognized economic scholar under the Imperial regime, continued his studies as a Soviet citizen after 1917. A doctor of political economy and statistics, he has taught at several Soviet universities. He is a Corresponding Member of the USSR Academy of Science and a Member of the Ukrainian Academy of Science. His numerous articles and books have brought him many honors, including a Stalin prize received in 1949. The work from which the following excerpt is taken was first published in 1939 and received official approval for use as a textbook in Soviet institutions of higher education. As the student will see, it is very much a Marxian interpretation.

THE WAR AND THE MILITARIZATION OF RUSSIAN INDUSTRY

The war disrupted both industry and agriculture by altering all normal conditions of production, demand, export, manpower, and other factors. Owing to the heavy mobilization of workers, the output of industries working for the free market began to decline seriously by early 1915. The position of industry was affected quite radically by the militarization of industry and by the conversion of plants to war requirements, which was at first performed through the private initiative of the entrepreneurs interested in obtaining profitable government orders, and afterward by official compulsion. By the autumn of 1914, military orders had absorbed all facilities of the larger metal-processing and metal-construction plants: the Sormovo, the Bryansk, the Kolomna, and others. As a result, production of locomotives at the Sormovo Plant, for example, dropped from 117 in 1913 to 64 in 1916 and to 55 in 1917. From 1915 all more or less suitable metal-processing plants began to be converted for war production, with little quantitative or qualitative results, however, owing to the inflexi-

bility and poor technical equipment of these plants. The same was attempted, with even less success, in the chemical industry, which was converted to the production of explosives and similar military supplies.

These were followed by the leather and shoe industry, and the cotton and wool industries, which were adapted to the production of supplies ordered by the military commissaries.

The results of the first year of war production were quite depressing. By the spring of 1915 it had become obvious that Russian industry was incapable of coping with the tremendous military problems imposed by the world imperialist war. . . .

. . . The low technical equipment of the country's industry, especially in the production of machines and weapons, precluded the possibility of effecting the necessary retooling of its plants for new types of production once imports of machinery from abroad ceased. On the eve of the war, of a total annual consumption of 720 million rubles in technical equipment of capitalist industry, up to 37 per cent was satisfied by imports from abroad, and in the case of industrial machinery, as much as 58 per

From Peter I. Lyashchenko, *History of the National Economy of Russia to the 1917 Revolution*, pp. 758–68, 771–72, 773–77. By permission of The Macmillan Co. Copyright 1949 by The American Council of Learned Societies.

cent. In addition the acute shortage of qualified workers, the congestion of transport, the critical condition of the fuel supply, and the general disruption that was steadily spreading throughout all economic and public life completed the hopelessness of the situation. As a result many enterprises were forced to liquidate, and although war conditions gave rise to new industrial undertakings, the number of liquidated companies exceeded the number of those newly established.

Thus 350 enterprises closed as early as 1914 compared to 215 new establishments. In 1915 these figures were 573 closed and 187 newly opened, in 1916, 298 closed and 276 opened, and in 1917, 541 closed compared with 264 opened. The militarization of industry and "survival of the fittest" among enterprises naturally resulted in further concentration of industry. Hence some quantitative successes were achieved in the increase of production. The "war" industries succeeded in increasing their production somewhat by 1916. According to the industrialists' own figures, in one of the main regions engaged in "defense work," the fifteen provinces of the central-industrial region, the number of workers increased by 19 per cent in 1916 compared with the prewar period, and in the metal-processing industry of that region specifically, the increase amounted to 190 per cent, chiefly as a result of attracting unskilled manpower. The situation was similar in the metal-processing industries of the Petrograd and the Ural regions. Conditions were much worse, however, in the branches of industry not working on war orders. . . .

The most catastrophic influence upon the national economy and in undermining the country's basic production forces was not so much the decline in output but complete absorption in war production. The militarized industry siphoned from the economic life of the country everything available: metal, fuel, financial resources, and manpower. According to the figures of the War Industries Committee, the country's

ferrous metal requirements (which before the war amounted to 305 million poods[1]) in 1915 had to be satisfied with an allocation of 48 million poods for the private market and 15.8 million poods for industrial consumption of the total 241.3 million poods of iron produced. Among the various metal products of mass consumption, structural iron, for example, declined in output from 41 million poods to 15.7 million poods. The amount of orders received by the leading distribution syndicate, Prodamet, declined to 79 million poods of iron products of all types in 1916, and to about 48 million in 1917, compared with 148 million poods in 1913.

THE FUEL CRISIS

Similar results may be observed in the distribution of fuel. With respect to coal, even the expanded production of the Donets-basin region in 1916 could not cover all requirements because of the elimination of the Polish coal region and of the considerable foreign imports of the prewar period.

Fuel production during the war years was as follows (in million poods):

YEARS	COAL		PETROLEUM
	In the Whole Empire	Including the Donets Basin	
1913	2,199	1,560	561
1914	2,181	1,684	550
1915	1,919	1,627	568
1916	2,096	1,751	602

The increased Donets-basin output was not sufficient to compensate for the loss of the entire output of the Dombrovsky coal basin. In 1913 the latter yielded almost 426 million poods of the total coal output of 2,199 million poods, and in 1916 total production could not be raised above 2,096 million poods. Moreover, although a maximum labor supply was thrown into the Donets coal industry (291,000 persons by January, 1917, compared to 168,000 in 1913), production per worker declined by

[1] One pood equals 36 pounds. [Editor's note]

January, 1917, to 534 poods a month compared to 764 poods a month in 1913.

The situation with regard to petroleum was somewhat better, but here, too, production was far from adequate. The country's oil resources were exploited wastefully. With the increase of oil production in 1916, drilling work declined. By 1917 the number of active oil wells in the Baku region dropped from 3,600 to 1,500, drilling work having declined to about one-tenth of the usual volume. A similar tendency was apparent in the Grozny and Emba regions.

As a consequence of the war and of the mobilization of industry, the consumption of fuel increased to a great extent, especially because some of the country's major industrial regions formerly operating on imported coal were now drawing upon the domestic coal supply. The greatest detriment to industry was not so much the coal deficit as the policy of fuel distribution. The creation of a Special Council for Fuel, and its policy of fuel allocation based on the establishment of categories of privileged (entirely war-connected) and nonprivileged (all other) consumers, brought the country into a state of critical fuel scarcity.

THE CRISIS AND DECLINE IN AGRICULTURE

Most direct and most depressing was the effect of the war and the heavy manpower mobilization upon agriculture. Compared with the prewar army of 1,370,000 persons, Russia mobilized during the war, up to the middle of 1917, a total of 14 million persons. Moreover the first years of the war withdrew from the national economy about 7.4 million persons, most of them adult workers of the agricultural population. According to the census of 1917, no less than a third, and in some cases as much as one-half, of the total number of peasant households were left without workers in a majority of provinces. The forced labor of the war prisoners and refugees brought little relief both because of its limited supply and because of the casual manner in which this type of manpower was distributed. In all, not more than 10 per cent

of the losses in labor was replenished from the above source.

Aside from devouring great masses of human labor power, the war seriously undermined all resources of production in agriculture. As a result of the metal scarcity and the policy of distribution of fuel and metal, the production of agricultural machines and implements was thoroughly disrupted. By the end of 1914 some of the largest farm-machinery plants had reduced their output of machinery to one-third of the prewar level, while in 1916, production in 173 of the largest plants amounted to only 25 per cent of the prewar output of farm machines. A majority of these plants was converted to war production, while the remaining plants were allowed only 1.3 million poods of metal in lieu of the 15 million poods previously consumed. With a situation of this type prevailing in the large plants, the position of the small repair and maintenance workshops, the village forges, was obviously desperate: because of a lack of metal and fuel and because of the mobilization of manpower into the army, repair work on farm inventory was completely abandoned. Finally, to this should be added the almost complete halt in agricultural machinery imports, which before the war amounted to 9.7 million poods annually and covered about 50 per cent of the country's requirements; in 1915 only some 196,000 poods were imported, and 391,000 poods in 1916. Thus, with domestic production reduced to 20 or 25 per cent and imports to 4 per cent of the prewar level, only 8 to 9 per cent of the requirements for agricultural machinery was satisfied. Together with the loss of manpower in rural economy, this decline in farm machinery supply lowered output very seriously. A change in wartime economic policy during 1915–1917 (in 1917 some 1,726,000 poods of farm machines valued at 21.8 million rubles were imported from abroad) was too late to be effective. In any event it could not actually have saved the situation.

Another rather important factor, likewise

affected by the reduction of domestic output as well as imports, was mineral fertilizer
requirements. Of a total quantity of 42
million poods consumed before the war,
only about 11 million poods were produced
within the country, while 31 million poods
were imported from abroad, chiefly from
Germany. While imports dropped to almost zero, domestic production also declined
as a result of the conversion of the chemical
industry to war, with the result that in 1916
the market could satisfy no more than a
similar 8 to 9 per cent of consumption
needs. A similar situation existed in the
supply of improved seeds, which were
hitherto imported from abroad.

Finally, the war dealt a most serious blow
to another basic element in agricultural
production; namely, livestock. The mass
mobilization of horses from the peasant
economy, without regard for its minimum
needs of draft power, left a number of
households either without horses or with
too few. Altogether, in the second half of
1917 some 2.1 million head of horses were
mobilized, and the total number of work
horses in the fifty provinces of European
Russia declined from 17.9 million in 1914
to 12.8 million in 1917. No less disastrous
was the decline in draft cattle generally,
and in oxen particularly, caused by increased requisitioning and slaughtering for
the army food supply, which consumed
about 18 million head. On the whole,
taking into account the cattle lost in the
provinces occupied by the German Army,
the total losses in cattle during the first
nineteen months of the war amounted to
26 million head. The effect upon the
peasant economy was particularly ruinous,
since it was incapable of replenishing its
losses in livestock, of replacing its worn-out
inventory, or of alleviating the shortage of
manpower on the farm.

The result of this situation was a steep
decline in farm output of all types, especially in the more important market com-
modities as well as in grain. By 1917 the
acreage of the major grains declined to 78

million *dessyatins* compared to 88.6 million
in 1914, or by nearly 10 million *dessyatins*.[2]
The edible grains dropped from an acreage
of 51.2 million to 45.1 million *dessyatins*.
The sharpest decline occurred in the major
commercial and producing areas (the
North Caucasus and the southern steppe
provinces) and in the more valuable commercial grains, wheat and barley. With an
inevitable decline in yield, the gross harvest
of grain dropped even below the level of
the reduced acreage. The total harvest of
all grains and potatoes was 7 billion poods
during 1909–1913 and 6.9 billion in 1914,
declining in 1916 to 5.1 billion, and in
1917 to 5 billion poods; of this, the food
grains dropped from a total of 2.8 billion
poods during the last peacetime five-year
period to 2.2 billion poods for 1916–1917,
while the fodder grains (barley and oats)
declined from 2.1 billion poods for the
prewar period to 1.1 billion poods in 1916.

The exportation of agricultural products
was almost completely discontinued. . . .

THE FOOD CRISIS

Bearing in mind that before the war
grain exports alone withdrew from the
national food supply between 600 and 750
million poods, with the complete cessation
of exports the above-cited decline in harvest
should not have resulted in a food crisis.
However, by 1916 the country began to
experience a critical food shortage. The
causes lay not only in the above-mentioned
decline in agricultural production but also
in the entire combination of a disrupted
economic life and the government's food
and supply policy. By directing all industrial production into war channels, the
government policy deprived the village of
its supply of goods, of both the producer
and consumer type. The village lost interest
not only in planting but also in selling its
grain, especially when the value of the
currency began to decline in the face of an
increased output of paper money. Begin-

[2] One *dessyatin* equals 2.7 acres. [Editor's note]

ning with 1915 a food scarcity was clearly in evidence not only in the cities but in army provisioning as well.

In the fields of civilian food supply and of the regulation of agriculture and the agricultural market, an attempt was made, in view of the impossibility of coping with the difficulties by ordinary measures, to establish the same type of regulating agencies that existed in industry and in transport. In August, 1915, a Special Council on Food was established, formally endowed with consultative functions only but in reality invested with very broad, almost dictatorial authority in the person of the president and his local "delegates," the governors.

From this time the food procurement for the population (aside from army procurement, which remained under the control of the military authorities) passed into the hands of the government and partly to the local municipal and rural self-administrative agencies. The centralized government apparatus procured 305 million poods during 1914–1915, 502 million in 1915–1916, and 540 million poods in 1916–1917. In other words the government procurement took away nearly the entire volume of commercial grain, destroying the free grain market. A situation of this type was, however, far from a successful solution of the food crisis. Government procurement was based on a system of fixed farm prices, which, with the depreciation of the currency and the wide divergence between farm prices and the price of industrial goods, was very unsatisfactory from the standpoint of the agricultural producers. After partial requisitioning had also failed to alleviate the situation, it was decided in December, 1916, to undertake the compulsory allocation of grain, beginning with a pool of 772 million poods of grain. But this measure was not put into force before the coming of the February revolution. Upon the testimony of Shingarev, the first Minister for Food of the Provisional Government, the government had no grain reserves of any kind at its disposal by 1917, and in early March of 1917 "there were moments when the flour supply was sufficient for only a few days in Petrograd and Moscow, while there were sectors of the front with hundreds of thousands of soldiers where the bread supply was sufficient to last no more than half a day."

* * *

THE RISING COST OF LIVING

The decline in agricultural production, the disruption of supply, the reduction in consumer-goods output, and the rapid depreciation of the ruble could not fail to cause a rapid rise in the cost of living affecting all articles of consumption, especially foodstuffs. The burden of the high cost of living was made more real by the fact that the nominal increase in money wages, especially during the first years of the war, lagged far behind the rise of prices. The facts most responsible for this situation were the increased amount of currency in circulation and the depreciation of the paper money.

During the first few months of the war, as early as December, 1914, food prices increased by 25 per cent compared with the prewar level, while other prices rose by 11 per cent. Toward the spring of 1917, grain prices increased by 59 per cent and industrial goods by 35 per cent. During the second year of the war the price of grain rose by 122 per cent and that of industrial goods by 145 per cent. Finally, by 1917 prices on all goods increased in the course of one year from 40 to 200 per cent. Thus, if we take food prices in Moscow for 1916 as 100, the price index for January, 1917, would be: bread, 141; meat, 249; vegetables, 328; milk, 191; dairy products, 238; and so forth. The sharpest increase in food prices occurred in the major industrial and urban centers such as Petrograd, Moscow, and others. In Petrograd, prices in late 1916 increased in comparison with 1914: milk, 150 per cent; white bread, 500; butter, 830; shoes and clothing, 400 to 600 per cent.

THE CONDITION OF THE WORKERS

During the war of 1914–1917 the condition of the workers deteriorated substantially as a result of the gap between the wage level and the rising cost of living, poorer conditions of work, and wartime repression of labor, especially in the militarized enterprises. The workday was nearly everywhere lengthened, as a rule, by the compulsory overtime work necessary for the fulfillment of war orders. The number of rest days was reduced, and sanitary conditions at the plants grew worse as a result of overloading the factories and twenty-four-hour production, which increased sickness as well as accidents among the workers. With a great number of male workers recruited into the army, the manufacturers began to utilize a larger proportion of female and child labor, which, although less trained, was less costly. By 1916, despite the fact that industry had not been able to cope successfully with the huge orders placed by the army, unemployment began to increase not only in the textile industry, for example, but in metallurgical production as well. In 1915 the government organized labor exchanges in Petrograd and several other major centers. But during the nine months of their operation only 237,900 workers of the 313,900 workers offering their services obtained work. The industrialists preferred to hire, outside the labor-exchange channels, the cheaper, though less trained, labor of women and children, while the labor exchanges were accumulating masses of unemployed trained workers.

Wages, nominally increased during wartime, were in reality lagging behind the rise of prices. Average annual wages in the Moscow industrial region were as follows (in rubles):

YEARS	AVERAGE FOR ALL INDUSTRIES	METAL WORKERS	TEXTILE WORKERS
1913	218	384	210
1914	221	324	202
1915	248	445	221
1916	406	761	320

The nominal wage of all workers in the Moscow region increased by 86 per cent, that of the metal workers, by 98, and textile workers, by 65.6 per cent, but the price of goods had risen by the end of 1916 by 200 to 300 per cent as compared with 1914, and prices on articles of prime necessity in the worker's consumption rose to five or six times the prewar level. The budgetary costs of the worker as of January 1, 1917, had increased by 294 per cent on an average for all Russia, and by 306 per cent for Moscow, in comparison with 1913. Hence, despite a nominal increase in wages, the workers were on the verge of starvation in 1916. The attempt to place labor in the war industries on a system of payment in kind by the military authorities, along with other measures of the tsarist regime and the bourgeoisie for "combating the high cost of living," ended in failure. The workers soon began to realize that the solution of their "food problem" was to be found in a revolutionary struggle against tsarism and the imperialistic bourgeoisie.

THE LABOR MOVEMENT DURING THE WAR PERIOD

The military crisis and the disruption of the capitalist economy, which was turning more and more into a general economic, social, and political crisis, could not avoid intensifying and hastening the process of revolutionizing the toiling masses in general and, of course, the progressive ranks of the workers in particular. The war was, in Lenin's expression, "a mighty accelerator" of the process of revolutionization, despite the great quantitative and qualitative changes that occurred in the composition of the working class during the war.

The mobilization of 14 million peasants and workers for service at the front at once withdrew from production a considerable proportion of workers, frequently those best trained, and occasionally replaced them with politically less advanced elements. But this circumstance, which at times affected production unfavorably, was of tremendous political significance: it inten-sified the propagandistic work of the mobi-lized progressive workers at the front. At some plants the very first phases of mobili-zation withdrew about 40 per cent of the skilled labor. Although the government and the bourgeoisie had regarded mobiliza-tion of the workers as a device to discourage their revolutionary activity, economic neces-sity required that some skilled workers be left behind, especially in enterprises en-gaged in war production, which became systematic after the inauguration of a system of industrial mobilization.

Of particular political significance was the fact that, with the expansion and new construction of large plants, the concentra-tion of industry continued to increase still further during the war. Thus, of a total of 2.5 million industrial workers on Janu-ary 1, 1915, small enterprises employing up to 100 persons (78.4 per cent of all enter-prises) accounted for only 17.8 per cent of the labor force, while the larger enterprises, employing over 500 workers and constitut-ing only 5.6 per cent of the country's enter-prises, employed 56.5 per cent of all workers. These huge enterprises, chiefly in the metal-processing industry, became the labor head-quarters for the preparation of the revolu-tion.

During the first years following the declaration of war, mobilization provoked serious strikes and labor demonstrations at Petersburg. Because of the wartime regime, however, the labor movement and its leader-ship had to prepare a new set of tactics. Consequently, during the very first days of the war a type of propagandist-agitational work came into being, of which Lenin said, "It *alone* will bring the fruits of socialism and the fruits of the revolution." . . .

The rising cost of living and the food crisis could not but serve as revolutionary factors among the masses. The explanation of the political significance of the food problem to the worker became one of the most pertinent and easily understood issues, even for the less progressive masses. Gradu-ally the minor issues of food, the price of bread, and the lack of goods turned into general political discussions concerning the entire system of the social order. In this atmosphere political movements and politi-cal demands grew feverishly and matured quickly, although they were still limited in form to economic strikes.

The "food riots" that broke out in Petrograd and Moscow in April, 1915, slowly spread to various other centers and acquired a political character, laying the foundation for the future civil war. At that time Lenin already considered it necessary to utilize the food difficulties for spreading revolutionary ideas among the masses, so as to "explain to the masses . . . that we are in the presence of an historical impellent of the greatest force which generates disaster, famine, and countless miseries. This im-pellent is war."

The above statements with respect to the condition of the working class and of all toilers in general during the first years of the war, also explain the character of the labor movement during these years. Figures on the strike movement (at enterprises sub-ject to factory inspection) during the war years are presented in the following table:

YEARS	NUMBER OF STRIKES	NUMBER OF STRIKING WORKERS (Thousands)
1914 (August to December)	68	34.7
1915	928	539.5
1916	1,284	951.7
1917 (January and February)	1,330	676.3

The movement in the form of economic strikes was begun by the textile workers, while the final phase of the political strike movement was undertaken by the metal-workers. Petrograd became the center of the labor movement and of its more clearly expressed political demands. Here, begin-ning with the second half of 1915, the strikes had become more tempestuous in character, involving the introduction of political demands and active armed opposition to the police and the troops. By September, 1916, the commander of the Petrograd military district announced that workers who failed to appear at their jobs would be sent to courts-martial (that is, actually to the firing squad). But even this military repression failed to halt the movement.

Beginning with October, 1916, the labor movement of Petersburg and Moscow entered a period of widespread increase in political and revolutionary demands made under the direct leadership of the "Leninist underground" and by Bolshevik slogans and propaganda. During the first months of 1917, the proletariat of Petrograd emerged fully prepared to deliver the crushing blow to the tsarist regime, and, further, to the whole system of Russian capitalism.

On February 18, 1917, a strike broke out at Petrograd among the workers of the Putilov plants, and by February 22 the workers at most enterprises in the city were on strike. During February 23 and 24 the city witnessed a number of large political demonstrations, and about 200,000 workers were on strike. By February 25 and 26 the revolutionary movement had spread to all proletarian sections of Petrograd, and the demonstrations began to turn into attempts at an uprising.

In the other industrial centers, including Moscow, the movement was at first limited in scope, with purely economic demands foremost, but here, too, strikes provoked by the high cost of living and marked by purely economic demands evolved into significant political events as a result of the political leadership of the Bolsheviks and the resentment of the workers against military repression by the government. Among such events were the strikes at Kostroma and Ivanovo-Voznesensk in the summer of 1915, at the Tver mills, at the Tula and Bryansk plants in 1916, and at the Nizhny Novgorod factories, all of which ended only after troops fired upon the workers. In the south the labor movement had been developing with equal intensity since 1915–1916, changing rapidly even there, and for the same reasons, from economic forms of struggle to political demands and to active resistance against the police. Such were the strikes at the metallurgical enterprises of Taganrog, at the mines and pits of Mariupol and the Don districts, at the shipbuilding yards of Nikolayev, and at the mines and enterprises of the Bakhmut, Gorlovka, and Baku regions, which ended in bloody clashes. All these strikes, while originating for economic reasons and not always successful from the standpoint of the worker, were vastly significant because they prepared the working masses of the periphery for delivering, in conjunction with the Petrograd workers, the crushing blow against the tsarist regime.

The revolutionary struggle of the worker found sympathy and support among the soldier-peasants in uniform. Thus soldiers called to suppress a strike at the automobile plant of Louis Renault in Petrograd in October, 1916, fired not at the workers but at the police.

In the course of the February revolution, during the first days of the uprising (February 26) the Petrograd garrison joined the side of the revolutionary masses against the autocracy. On the morning of February 27 some 10,000 soldiers were in open rebellion, by the evening of the same day, over 60,000, and by the morning of March 1, 144,700. In the course of that day, as they became better acquainted with the situation, the military detachments of the capital became fully activated and changed to the side of the revolution. By the evening of March 1, 170,000 soldiers had risen against the government.

The March Revolution Was Spontaneous

WILLIAM H. CHAMBERLIN

William Henry Chamberlin is perhaps one of the best-known American authorities on the Russian Revolution. Born in Brooklyn in 1897 and
educated at Haverford College, he has had a long and brilliant career
as journalist, author, and historian. From 1922 through 1934 he was
Moscow correspondent of *The Christian Science Monitor,* an experience
which helped him gain deep insights into Russian problems. In more
recent years he has lectured at various universities, and he continues
to write regularly for several magazines. In *The Russian Revolution*
Chamberlin has tried hard to examine all the relevant sources and to
give a scrupulously unbiased report based on their evidence.

THE collapse of the Romanov autocracy in March 1917 was one of the most leaderless, spontaneous, anonymous revolutions of all time. While almost every thoughtful observer in Russia in the winter of 1916–1917 foresaw the likelihood of the crash of the existing regime no one, even among the revolutionary leaders, realized that the strikes and bread riots which broke out in Petrograd on March 8 would culminate in the mutiny of the garrison and the overthrow of the government four days later.

The Tsarina was not distinguished by political perspicacity; and it is not surprising that she should write to her husband, who was at the Headquarters of the General Staff in Moghilev, on March 10, when the capital was in the grip of a general strike: "This is a hooligan movement, young people run and shout that there is no bread, simply to create excitement, along with workers who prevent others from working. If the weather were very cold they would all probably stay at home. But all this will pass and become calm, if only the Duma will behave itself."

But it was not only the Tsarina who failed to see the impending storm. The Socialist Revolutionary Zenzinov declared: "The Revolution was a great and joyous surprise for us, revolutionaries, who had worked for it for years and had always expected it." The Menshevik Internationalist Sukhanov observes: "Not one party was prepared for the great overturn." The Bolshevik worker Kaourov, who took an active part in the Revolution, testifies that on March 8 "no one thought of such an imminent possibility of revolution." As for the leaders of the Duma, they might whisper among each other about the possibility of a palace *coup d'état;* but the last thing they desired was an uncontrolled movement from below.[1]

[1] *Socialist Revolutionary:* the peasant-oriented, agrarian-socialist (non-Marxist) party of which Victor Chernov was leader. The *Mensheviks* and *Bolsheviks* were mutually hostile parties which had developed from an earlier split in the Russian Social Democratic Labor Party. The Bolshevik party was characterized by a high degree of centralization and discipline under Lenin's leadership, and its political tactics were conspiratorial and aggressively revolutionary. The Mensheviks were loosely organized, less militant, and in general committed to an evolutionary interpretation of historical development which made them relatively passive after March, 1917. [Editor's note]

From William Henry Chamberlin, *The Russian Revolution, 1917–1921* (New York, 1952), I, 73–80.
Copyright 1935 by The Macmillan Co. and used with the publisher's permission.

Wartime circumstances alone made any effective guidance of a mass uprising impossible. The men who afterwards distinguished themselves in the Bolshevik Revolution were either living abroad, like Lenin and Trotzky and Zinoviev, or in prison or in Siberian exile, like Stalin, Kamenev and Dzerzhinsky. The more prominent leaders of other revolutionary parties were also absent from Petrograd in the decisive days. The Bolshevik members of the Duma had been exiled to Siberia in the first months of the War, and the Menshevik members of the War Industries Committee were arrested by the zealous Minister of the Interior, Protopopov, early in the year. There was a skeleton underground Bolshevik organization in Russia; but its activities were narrowly circumscribed by lack of experienced professional revolutionaries, lack of funds, and the all-pervading espionage. Indeed most of the members of the Bolshevik Petrograd Party Committee were arrested at a critical moment in the development of the movement, on the morning of March 11.

So the police measures for the protection of the Tsarist regime were almost perfect. At first sight and on paper the military measures seemed equally imposing. Petrograd had a huge garrison of about 160,000 soldiers. To be sure the fighting quality of this garrison, as subsequent events were to prove, was in inverse ratio to its size. The original Guard regiments had been sent to the front (a grave strategic error, from the standpoint of the internal security of the old regime); and the troops quartered in Petrograd consisted mainly of new recruits, untrained, housed in crowded barracks, often poorly fed.

But the Tsarist authorities did not rely primarily on the unwieldy garrison for the suppression of any possible uprising. The Minister of the Interior, Protopopov, proposed to operate against insurgent throngs first with police, then with Cossack cavalry units, bringing troops into operation only in the last resort. An elaborate plan for the suppression of disorder in the capital had been submitted to the Tsar in January. A combined force of 12,000 troops, gendarmes and police was created for this specific purpose; and a military commander was appointed in each of the six police districts into which the city was divided.

Military preparations, therefore, had not been neglected, even if there were serious omissions, quite consistent with the frequently slipshod character of Tsarist administration, in paying little attention to the morale of the troops in the capital and in selecting as commander of the Petrograd Military District, General Khabalov, a man of little experience in commanding troops in actual military operations. The unforeseen circumstances that upset all the governmental calculations were the stubbornness of the demonstrators and the ultimate unreliability of the garrison.

The atmosphere of Petrograd was so charged with discontent in this third winter of an unsuccessful war that very slight causes were sufficient to bring about a formidable explosion. There had been intermittent strikes throughout January and February. Although there was not an absolute shortage of bread poor transportation and faulty distribution made it necessary for the workers and their wives, in many cases, to stand in long queues for bread and other products. The poorer classes of the city were not apathetic from actual hunger; but they were angry and annoyed at the growing cost of living and the other deprivations which the War brought with it. Something of a sense of crowd psychology, of a sense of massed power must have developed also, from the noteworthy growth in the number of industrial workers up to approximately 400,000 as a result of the presence of many war industry plants in the capital.

The movement that was to end in the overthrow of the Romanov dynasty started on March 8, which is observed by Socialist parties as Women's Day. After speeches in the factories crowds of women poured out on the streets, especially in the workingclass Viborg section of the city, clamoring for bread. Here and there red flags appeared with inscriptions: "Down with Autocracy." There were occasional clashes with the police; but the day passed off without serious conflicts. Almost ninety thousand workers struck and fifty factories were closed. A circumstance that enhanced the militant mood of the demonstrators was a lockout at the large Putilov metal works. The workers of this plant were proverbially turbulent, with a long record of strikes; and when a wage dispute had come up in one department the management on March 7 declared a general lockout. So a coincidence of three factors — the dissatisfaction with the food situation, the celebration of Women's Day and the Putilov labor dispute, which let loose over twenty thousand workers for active participation in the demonstration — combined to give the first impetus to the Revolution.

The movement gained in scope and intensity on March 9, when the number of strikers was estimated at 197,000. There was a concerted drive by the workers to reach the central part of the city. Although the police guarded the bridges over the Neva, which was to some extent a boundary between the workingclass and the governmental parts of the city, it was relatively easy to cross the river on the ice, and meetings and demonstrations were held in the centre of the capital. An ominous symptom for the government appeared: the Cossacks showed little energy in breaking up the crowds. So a Cossack squadron rode off, amid loud cheers, leaving undisturbed a revolutionary gathering on the Nevsky Prospect, the main boulevard of Petrograd; and the police reports of the day note an incident on Znamenskaya Square, when the Cossacks responded with bows to the applause of a throng which they did not disperse.

Attacks on the police became more common on this second day of the movement, the mobs using as weapons lumps of ice, cobblestones, heavy sticks. However, firearms were not used in suppressing the disorder and there was still no general

conviction of an impending crisis. The British Ambassador, Sir George Buchanan. telegraphed to Foreign Minister Balfour: "Some disorders occurred to-day, but nothing serious."

The 10th witnessed to a large extent a repetition of the events of the 9th, but on a larger scale. The strike became general; newspapers ceased to appear; the students in the universities abandoned their studies. The numbers both of the demonstrators and of the forces employed by the government increased; and there was a longer casualty list on both sides. Although there was still no mutiny, insubordination and passivity on the part of the troops, especially of the Cossacks, were more noticeable. On Znamenskaya Square a Cossack even cut down a police lieutenant, Krilov, with his sabre. The instinctive strategy of the crowd adapted itself to the mood of the troops. While there were fierce attacks on the police (by this time the police in the riotous Viborg district no longer ventured to appear on the streets, but were barricaded in their stations) there was an attempt to conciliate the troops and to avoid provoking them.

So far as there was organized leadership in the movement it aimed at winning over the troops, rather than at arming the workers. So the Bolshevik Shlyapnikov, one of the three members of the Bureau of the Central Committee of the Party, tells how he opposed the more hotheaded workers who continually demanded arms, or at least revolvers: "I decisively refused to search for arms at all and demanded that the soldiers should be drawn into the uprising, so as to get arms for all the workers. This was more difficult than to get a few dozen revolvers; but in this was the whole programme of action."

These three days of turmoil naturally affected the national and local legislative bodies, the Duma and the Petrograd City Council; and speeches were made demanding the appointment of a ministry responsible to the Duma. The Laborite deputy and radical lawyer Alexander Kerensky, destined to play a leading part in subsequent months, attacked the government so sharply in the Duma on the 9th that the Tsarina expressed a fervent desire that he should be hanged. These speeches, however, had little effect on the movement, because the War Minister forbade their publication, and after the morning of March 10, newspapers ceased to appear as a result of the general strike.

General Khabalov on March 10 received a peremptory telegram from the Tsar worded as follows: "I command you to suppress from tomorrow all disorders on the streets of the capital, which are impermissible at a time when the fatherland is carrying on a difficult war with Germany." This imperial order caused a sharp change in the tactics of the Petrograd authorities. Hitherto the use of firearms had been avoided. On the night of the 10th Khabalov gave his subordinate officers instructions to fire on crowds which refused to disperse after warning. This was the decisive stake of the old regime. If the troops obeyed, the revolutionary movement would be crushed. If they did not obey . . . But this alternative was apparently not considered very seriously.

As a further sign of resolute action the police on the night of the 10th arrested about a hundred persons suspected of holding seditious views, including five members of the Petrograd Committee of the Bolshevik Party. On the surface the course of events on the 11th, which was a Sunday, represented a victory for the government. There was firing on the crowds in four separate places in the central part of the city; and on Znamenskaya Square the training detachment of the Volinsky regiment used machine-guns as well as rifles, with the result that about forty persons were killed and an equal number were wounded. Toward evening there was an outburst of rebellion in one company of the Pavlovsk regiment; but it was put down with the aid of other troops, and the ringleaders were imprisoned in the fortress of Peter and Paul. The government, which was headed by Prince Golitzin as Premier, apparently

felt in a stronger position, because in the evening it adopted a decision to dissolve the Duma, thereby breaking off the half-hearted negotiations which had hitherto been carried on with the President of the Duma, Rodzianko, about possible coöperation between the Ministry and the Duma.

Rodzianko decided to try the effect of a personal appeal to the Tsar and despatched a telegram containing the following gravely warning phrases: "The situation is serious. There is anarchy in the capital. The government is paralyzed. It is necessary immediately to entrust a person who enjoys the confidence of the country with the formation of the government. Any delay is equivalent to death. I pray God that in this hour responsibility will not fall on the sovereign."

But neither this telegram, nor the still more urgent message which Rodzianko sent on the following morning, when the mutiny of the garrison was an accomplished fact, produced any impression on Nicholas II. Rodzianko's second telegram described the growing revolt and ended: "The situation is growing worse. Measures must be adopted immediately, because tomorrow will be too late. The last hour has come, when the fate of the fatherland and the dynasty is being decided."

After reading this message the Tsar impatiently remarked to his Minister of the Court, Count Fredericks: "This fat Rodzianko has written me some nonsense, to which I will not even reply."

There is a double significance in these last urgent appeals of the President of the Duma to the Tsar and especially in his instinctive employment of the phrase "The situation is growing worse," at a moment when the revolution was moving to victory. Like the great majority of the members of the Duma Rodzianko, who was himself a well-to-do landowner, desired to see the monarchy reformed, but not abolished. All Rodzianko's actions in these turbulent days were motivated by two factors: his hope, up to the last moment, that the Tsar would save himself and the monarchical principle by making necessary concessions, and his fear that the revolutionary movement would get out of hand.

The decisive hour of the Revolution struck on the morning of March 12, when the centre of attention shifts from rebellious workers with sticks and stones and bottles to insurgent soldiers with rifles and machine-guns. The firing on the crowds on Sunday, the 11th, was the snapping point in the frail cord of discipline that held the garrison of the capital. The mutiny that was to transform the prolonged street demonstrations into a genuine revolution started in the very unit which had inflicted the heaviest losses on the demonstrating crowds: the training detachment of the Volinsky regiment. During the night the soldiers discussed their impressions of the day's shooting and agreed that they would no longer fire on the crowds. When Captain Lashkevitch appeared in the barracks of the detachment on the morning of the 12th he was greeted with shouts: "We will not shoot." He read the telegram of the Tsar, demanding the suppression of the disorders; but this only aggravated the situation. Ultimately Lashkevitch either was shot by the insurgent soldiers or committed suicide; and the troops poured out into the streets under the command of Sergeant Kirpichnikov, one of the many obscure leaders of this unplanned upheaval. They soon aroused the soldiers of the Preobrazhensky and Litovsky regiments, who were quartered in nearby barracks.

Quickly brushing aside the resistance which some officers of the Moscow Regiment endeavored to offer and gaining new recruits among the soldiers of the Moscow regiment for their ranks, the swollen mass of soldiers made for the Viborg District, where they quickly fraternized with the throngs of workers and joined them in hunting down the police and breaking into arsenals, where the workers quickly secured the desired arms.

Khabalov, a weak and incompetent man at best, was thunderstruck as the news of one mutiny after another poured in on him.

He formed a supposedly loyal force of six companies under the command of Colonel Kutepov, but it simply melted away as soon as it came into contact with the revolutionary mobs. This largely psychological process of "melting away" recurred, incidentally, whenever there was an attempt to send "reliable" troops against the revolutionary capital. It explains why a movement without organized leadership was nevertheless invincible. This breakdown of normal military discipline cannot be attributed to any single precise cause. It was a compound of many things: war-weariness, hatred of the hard and often humiliating conditions of Russian army service, responsiveness to the general mood of discontent in the country — all explosive stuff that was ignited by the stubborn demonstrations of the workingclass population of Petrograd.

There are two features of the March Revolution that strike the observer again and again. There is the lack of planned leadership, and there is the action of the soldiers independently of their officers. The latter, with very few exceptions, simply disappeared during the decisive hours of the uprising. This fact inevitably exerted a profound effect on the subsequent morale and psychology of the soldiers, who followed leaders from their own ranks, often sergeants and corporals.

Khabalov, with the rapidly thinning remnant of his loyal troops, took refuge in the Winter Palace, where his forces on the afternoon of the 12th were reduced to "fifteen hundred or two thousand men, with a very small reserve of bullets." At the insistence of the Grand Duke Michael, the Tsar's brother, the Winter Palace was evacuated and the last defenders of the old regime took refuge in the neighboring Admiralty, whence they quietly dispersed on the following morning.

So the city passed completely into the hands of the revolutionaries. The accounts of many eyewitnesses of the upheaval are pervaded with a spirit of chaotic exaltation. The monarchy had fallen; and in the masses of the population there were few who mourned it. Vast throngs gathered to watch the burning of the large District Court building and adjoining prison; and the Tauride Palace, where the Duma held its sessions, was a magnet for endless throngs of soldiers, workers, students and curious spectators of all classes. Red bands and ribbons appeared as if by magic; and trucks filled with soldiers raced through the city, with their guns levelled against non-existent enemies. Except for the police, who were given short shrift when they were discovered hiding in garrets or firing from roofs on the crowds, the Revolution, although tumultuous, was, in the main, good-natured. There were relatively few excesses, surprisingly few, if one considers that common criminals were released indiscriminately with political offenders in the prisons which were stormed by the mobs. Class lines had not begun to assume their subsequent sharpness. An atmosphere of vague,

formless good-fellowship was prevalent; and the nationalist speeches of Shulgin or Rodzianko evoked the same hearty "Hurrah" as the exhortations of the revolutionary orators. The great mass of the mutinous soldiers scarcely realized what they were doing and were uncertain whether in the end they would be treated as heroes or as criminals.

The anonymous host of workers in collarless blouses and soldiers in grey uniforms overthrew the Romanov dynasty, with its three centuries of absolute rule behind it. But the rebellious mass had nothing concrete to put in the place of the old order. The efforts to form a new government inevitably revolved around the Duma, which, despite its lack of representative character and the timidity which it displayed in its dealings with the monarchy, was the sole national assembly in existence at the time of the Revolution.

Bolshevik Workingmen Led the Revolt

LEON TROTSKY

Leon Trotsky, born near Odessa in 1879, early became a professional revolutionary and remained in this profession until his assassination in Mexico in 1940. During an almost feverishly busy life he was a leading Marxian theoretician, a gifted and prolific journalist, a successful revolutionary, organizer of the Red Armies, and a high Soviet government official. A leader of the 1905 revolution, he joined the Bolshevik party in 1917 and was one of the chief organizers of the Bolshevik seizure— second in importance only to Lenin. During all his mature years, no matter what other great events gripped his attention, Trotsky wrote— speeches and orders, articles, books, and scholarly studies—all of them highly controversial, all of them brilliant. In the *History of the Russian Revolution,* from which a chapter is printed below, Trotsky describes with inimitable verve and detail his views on the leadership of the March Revolution.

LAWYERS and journalists belonging to the classes damaged by the revolution wasted a good deal of ink subsequently trying to prove that what happened in February was essentially a petticoat rebellion, backed up afterwards by a soldiers' mutiny and given out for a revolution. Louis XVI in his day also tried to think that the capture of the Bastille was a rebellion, but they respectfully explained to him that it was a revolution. Those who lose by a revolution are rarely inclined to call it by its real name. For that name, in spite of the efforts of spiteful reactionaries, is surrounded in the historic memory of mankind with a halo of liberation from all shackles and all prejudices. The privileged classes of every age, as also their lackeys, have always tried to declare the revolution which overthrew them, in contrast to past revolutions, a mutiny, a riot, a revolt of the rabble. Classes which have outlived themselves are not distinguished by originality.

Soon after the 27th of February attempts were also made to liken the revolution to the military coup d'état of the Young Turks, of which, as we know, they had been dreaming not a little in the upper circles of the Russian bourgeoisie. This comparison was so hopeless, however, that it was seriously opposed even in one of the bourgeois papers. Tugan-Baranovsky, an economist who had studied Marx in his youth, a Russian variety of Sombart, wrote on March 10 in the *Birzhevoe Vedomosti:*

The Turkish revolution consisted in a victorious uprising of the army, prepared and carried out by the leaders of the army; the soldiers were merely obedient executives of the plans of their officers. But the regiments of the Guard which on February 27 overthrew the Russian throne, came without their officers . . . Not the army but the workers began the insurrection; not the generals but the soldiers came to the State Duma. The soldiers supported the workers not because they were obediently fulfilling the commands of their officers, but because . . . they felt themselves blood brothers of the workers as a class composed of toilers like themselves. The peasants and the workers —those are the two social classes which made the Russian revolution.

From Leon Trotsky, *The History of the Russian Revolution,* translated by Max Eastman (3 vols., Simon & Schuster, 1936), I, 136–152. Reprinted by permission of Max Shachtman.

These words require neither correction, nor supplement. The further development of the revolution sufficiently confirmed and reënforced their meaning. In Petrograd the last day of February was the first day after the victory: a day of raptures, embraces, joyful tears, voluble outpourings; but at the same time a day of final blows at the enemy. Shots were still crackling in the streets. It was said that Protopopov's Pharaohs, not informed of the people's victory, were still shooting from the roofs. From below they were firing into attics, false windows and belfries where the armed phantoms of tzarism might still be lurking. About four o'clock they occupied the Admiralty where the last remnants of what was formerly the state power had taken refuge. Revolutionary organizations and improvised groups were making arrests throughout the town. The Schlüsselburg hard-labor prison was taken without a shot. More and more regiments were joining the revolution, both in the capital and in the environs.

The overturn in Moscow was only an echo of the insurrection in Petrograd. The same moods among the workers and soldiers, but less clearly expressed. A slightly more leftward tendency among the bourgeoisie. A still greater weakness among the revolutionary organizations than in Petrograd. When the events began on the Neva, the Moscow radical intelligentsia called a conference on the question what to do, and came to no conclusion. Only on the 27th of February strikes began in the shops and factories of Moscow, and then demonstrations. The officers told the soldiers in the barracks that a rabble was rioting in the streets and they must be put down. "But by this time," relates the soldier Shishilin, "the soldiers understood the word rabble in the opposite sense." Toward two o'clock there arrived at the building of the city duma many soldiers of various regiments inquiring how to join the revolution. On the next day the strikes increased. Crowds flowed toward the duma with flags. A soldier of an automobile company, Muralov,

an old Bolshevik, an agriculturist, a good-natured and courageous giant, brought to the duma the first complete and disciplined military detachment, which occupied the wireless station and other points. Eight months later Muralov will be in command of the troops of the Moscow military district.

The prisons were opened. The same Muralov was driving an automobile truck filled with freed political prisoners: a police officer with his hand at his vizor asked the revolutionist whether it was advisable to let out the Jews also. Dzerzhinsky, just liberated from a hard labor prison and without changing his prison dress, spoke in the duma building where a soviet of deputies was already formed. The artillerist Dorofeev relates how on March 1 workers from the Siou candy factory came with banners to the barracks of an artillery brigade to fraternize with the soldiers, and how many could not contain their joy, and wept. There were cases of sniping in the town, but in general neither armed encounters nor casualties: Petrograd answered for Moscow.

In a series of provincial cities the movement began only on March 1, after the revolution was already achieved even in Moscow. In Tver the workers went from their work to the barracks in a procession and having mixed with the soldiers marched through the streets of the city. At that time they were still singing the "Marseillaise," not the "International." In Nizhni-Novgorod thousands of workers gathered round the city duma building, which in a majority of the cities played the rôle of the Tauride Palace. After a speech from the mayor the workers marched off with red banners to free the politicals from the jails. By evening, eighteen out of the twenty-one military divisions of the garrison had voluntarily come over to the revolution. In Samara and Saratov meetings were held, soviets of workers' deputies organized. In Kharkov the chief of police, having gone to the railroad station and got news of the revolution, stood up in his carriage before an excited crowd and, lifting his hat, shouted at the top of his lungs: "Long live the revolution. Hurrah!" The news came to Ekaterinoslav from Kharkov. At the head of the demonstration strode the assistant chief of police carrying in his hand a long saber as in the grand parades on saints' days. When it became finally clear that the monarchy could not rise, they began cautiously to remove the tzar's portraits from the government institutions and hide them in the attics. Anecdotes about this, both authentic and imaginary, were much passed around in liberal circles, where they had not yet lost a taste for the jocular tone when speaking of the revolution. The workers, and the soldier barracks as well, took the events in a very different way. As to a series of other provincial cities (Pskov, Orel, Rybinsk, Penza, Kazan, Tzaritsyn, and others), the *Chronicle* remarks under date of March 2: "News came of the uprising and the population joined the revolution." This description, notwithstanding its summary character, tells with fundamental truth what happened.

News of the revolution trickled into the villages from the near-by cities, partly through the authorities, but chiefly through the markets, the workers, the soldiers on furlough. The villages accepted the revolution more slowly and less enthusiastically than the cities, but felt it no less deeply. For them it was bound up with the question of war and land.

It would be no exaggeration to say that Petrograd achieved the February revolution. The rest of the country adhered to it. There was no struggle anywhere except in Petrograd. There were not to be found anywhere in the country any groups of the population, any parties, institutions, or military units which were ready to put up a fight for the old régime. This shows how ill-founded was the belated talk of the reactionaries to the effect that if there had been cavalry of the Guard in the Petersburg garrison, or if Ivanov had brought a reliable brigade from the front, the fate of the monarchy would have been different.

Neither at the front nor at the rear was there a brigade or regiment to be found which was prepared to do battle for Nicholas II.

The revolution was carried out upon the initiative and by the strength of one city, constituting approximately about 1/75 of the population of the country. You may say, if you will, that this most gigantic democratic act was achieved in a most undemocratic manner. The whole country was placed before a *fait accompli*. The fact that a Constituent Assembly was in prospect does not alter the matter, for the dates and methods of convoking this national representation were determined by institutions which issued from the victorious insurrection of Petrograd. This casts a sharp light on the question of the function of democratic forms in general, and in a revolutionary epoch in particular. Revolutions have always struck such blows at the judicial fetishism of the popular will, and the blows have been more ruthless the deeper, bolder, and more democratic the revolutions.

It is often said, especially in regard to the great French revolution, that the extreme centralization of a monarchy subsequently permits the revolutionary capital to think and act for the whole country. That explanation is superficial. If revolutions reveal a centralizing tendency, this is not in imitation of overthrown monarchies, but in consequence of irresistible demands of the new society, which cannot reconcile itself to particularism. If the capital plays as dominating a rôle in a revolution as though it concentrated in itself the will of the nation, that is simply because the capital expresses most clearly and thoroughly the fundamental tendencies of the new society. The provinces accept the steps taken by the capital as their own intentions already materialized. In the initiatory rôle of the centers there is no violation of democracy, but rather its dynamic realization. However, the rhythm of this dynamic has never in great revolutions coincided with the rhythm of formal representative democracy. The provinces adhere to the activity of the center, but belatedly. With the swift development of events characteristic of a revolution this produces sharp crises in revolutionary parliamentarism, which cannot be resolved by the methods of democracy. In all genuine revolutions the national representation has invariably come into conflict with the dynamic force of the revolution, whose principal seat has been the capital. It was so in the seventeenth century in England, in the eighteenth in France, in the twentieth in Russia. The rôle of the capital is determined not by the tradition of a bureaucratic centralism, but by the situation of the leading revolutionary class, whose vanguard is naturally concentrated in the chief city: this is equally true for the bourgeoisie and the proletariat.

When the February victory was fully confirmed, they began to count up the victims. In Petrograd they counted 1443 killed and wounded, 869 of them soldiers, and 60 of these officers. By comparison with the victims of any battle in the Great Slaughter these figures are suggestively tiny. The liberal press declared the February revolution bloodless. In the days of general salubrity and mutual amnesty of the patriotic parties, nobody took the trouble to establish the truth. Albert Thomas,[1] a friend of everything victorious, even a victorious insurrection, wrote at that time about the "sunniest, most holiday-like, most bloodless Russian revolution." To be sure, he was hopeful that this revolution would remain at the disposal of the French Bourse. But after all Thomas did not invent this habit. On the 27th of June 1789, Mirabeau exclaimed: "How fortunate that this great revolution will succeed without evil-doing and without tears! . . . History has too long been telling us only of the actions of beasts of prey. . . . We may well hope that we are beginning the history of human beings." When all the three estates were united in the National Assembly the ancestors of Albert Thomas wrote: "The revolution is

ended. It has not cost a drop of blood." We must acknowledge, however, that at that period blood had really not yet flowed. Not so in the February days. Nevertheless the legend of a bloodless revolution stubbornly persisted, answering the need of the liberal bourgeois to make things look as though the power had come to him of its own accord.

Although the February revolution was far from bloodless, still one cannot but be amazed at the insignificant number of victims, not only at the moment of revolution but still more in the first period after it. This revolution, we must remember, was a paying-back for oppression, persecution, taunts, vile blows, suffered by the masses of the Russian people throughout the ages! The sailors and soldiers did in some places, to be sure, take summary revenge upon the most contemptible torturers in the person of their officers, but the number of these acts of settlement was at first insignificant in comparison with the number of the old bloody insults. The masses shook off their good-naturedness only a good while later, when they were convinced that the ruling classes wanted to drag everything back and appropriate to themselves a revolution not achieved by them, just as they had always appropriated the good things of life not produced by themselves.

*   *   *

Tugan-Baranovsky is right when he says that the February revolution was accomplished by workers and peasants — the latter in the person of the soldiers. But there still remains the great question: Who led the revolution? Who raised the workers to their feet? Who brought the soldiers into the streets? After the victory these questions became a subject of party conflict. They were solved most simply by the universal formula: Nobody led the revolution, it happened of itself. The theory of "spontaneousness" fell in most opportunely with the minds not only of all those gentlemen who had yesterday been peacefully governing, judging, convicting, defending, trad-

[1] French Socialist. [Editor's note]

ing, or commanding, and today were hastening to make up to the revolution, but also of many professional politicians and former revolutionists, who having slept through the revolution wished to think that in this they were not different from all the rest.

In his curious *History of the Russian Disorders,* General Denikin, former commander of the White Army, says of the 27th of February: "On that decisive day there were no leaders, there were only the elements. In their threatening current there were then visible neither aims, nor plans, nor slogans." The learned historian Miliukov delves no deeper than this general with a passion for letters. Before the revolution the liberal leader had declared every thought of revolution a suggestion of the German Staff. But the situation was more complicated after a revolution which had brought the liberals to power. Miliukov's task was now not to dishonor the revolution with a Hohenzollern origin, but on the contrary to withhold the honor of its initiation from revolutionists. Liberalism therefore has whole-heartedly fathered the theory of a spontaneous and impersonal revolution. Miliukov sympathetically cites the semiliberal, semi-socialist Stankevich, a university instructor who became Political Commissar at the headquarters of the Supreme Command: "The masses moved of themselves, obeying some unaccountable inner summons . . ." writes Stankevich of the February days. "With what slogans did the soldiers come out? Who led them when they conquered Petrograd, when they burned the District Court? Not a political idea, not a revolutionary slogan, not a conspiracy, and not a revolt, but a spontaneous movement suddenly consuming the entire old power to the last remnant." Spontaneousness here acquires an almost mystic character.

This same Stankevich offers a piece of testimony in the highest degree valuable: "At the end of January, I happened in a very intimate circle to meet with Kerensky. . . . To the possibility of a popular uprising they all took a definitely negative position, fearing lest a popular mass movement once aroused might get into an extreme leftward channel and this would create vast difficulties in the conduct of the war." The views of Kerensky's circle in nowise essentially differed from those of the Kadets. The initiative certainly did not come from there.

"The revolution fell like thunder out of the sky," says the president of the Social Revolutionary Party, Zenzinov. "Let us be frank: it arrived joyfully unexpected for us too, revolutionists who had worked for it through long years and waited for it always."

It was not much better with the Mensheviks. One of the journalists of the bourgeois emigration tells about his meeting in a tramcar on February 21 with Skobelev, a future minister of the revolutionary government: "This Social Democrat, one of the leaders of the movement, told me that the disorders had the character of plundering which it was necessary to put down. This did not prevent Skobelev from asserting a month later that he and his friends had made the revolution." The colors here are probably laid on a little thick, but fundamentally the position of the legal Social Democrats, the Mensheviks, is conveyed accurately enough.

Finally, one of the most recent leaders of the left wing of the Social Revolutionaries, Mstislavsky, who subsequently went over to the Bolsheviks, says of the February uprising: "The revolution caught us, the party people of those days, like the foolish virgins of the Bible, napping." It does not matter how much they resembled virgins, but it is true they were all fast asleep.

How was it with the Bolsheviks? This we have in part already seen. The principal leaders of the underground Bolshevik organization were at that time three men: the former workers Shliapnikov and Zalutsky, and the former student Molotov. Shliapnikov, having lived for some time abroad and in close association with Lenin, was in a political sense the most mature and active of these three who constituted the Bureau of the Central Committee. However, Shliapnikov's own memoirs best of all confirm the fact that the events were too much for the trio. Up to the very last hour these leaders thought that it was a question of a revolutionary manifestation, one among many, and not at all of an armed insurrection. Our friend Kayurov, one of the leaders of the Vyborg section, asserts categorically: "Absolutely no guiding initiative from the party centers was felt . . . the Petrograd Committee had been arrested and the representative of the Central Committee, Comrade Shliapnikov, was unable to give any directives for the coming day."

The weakness of the underground organizations was a direct result of police raids, which had given exceptional results amid the patriotic moods at the beginning of the war. Every organization, the revolutionary included, has a tendency to fall behind its social basis. The underground organization of the Bolsheviks at the beginning of 1917 had not yet recovered from its oppressed and scattered condition, whereas in the masses the patriotic hysteria had been abruptly replaced by revolutionary indignation.

In order to get a clear conception of the situation in the sphere of revolutionary leadership it is necessary to remember that the most authoritative revolutionists, the leaders of the left parties, were abroad and, some of them, in prison and exile. The more dangerous a party was to the old régime, the more cruelly beheaded it appeared at the moment of revolution. The Narodniks had a Duma faction headed by the non-party radical Kerensky.[2] The official leader of the Social-Revolutionaries, Chernov, was abroad. The Mensheviks had

a party faction in the Duma headed by Cheidze and Skobelev; Martov was abroad; Dan and Tseretelli, in exile. A considerable number of socialistic intellectuals with a revolutionary past were grouped around these left factions — Narodnik and Menshevik. This constituted a kind of political staff, but one which was capable of coming to the front only after the victory. The Bolsheviks had no Duma faction: their five worker-deputies, in whom the tzarist government had seen the organizing center of the revolution, had been arrested during the first few months of the war. Lenin was abroad, Zinoviev with him; Kamenev was in exile; in exile also, the then little known practical leaders: Sverdlov, Rykov, Stalin. The Polish social-democrat, Dzerzhinsky, who did not yet belong to the Bolsheviks, was at hard labor. The leaders accidentally present, for the very reason that they had been accustomed to act under unconditionally authoritative supervisors, did not consider themselves and were not considered by others capable of playing a guiding rôle in revolutionary events.

But if the Bolshevik Party could not guarantee the insurrection an authoritative leadership, there is no use talking of other organizations. This fact has strengthened the current conviction as to the spontaneous character of the February revolution. Nevertheless the conviction is deeply mistaken, or at least meaningless.

The struggle in the capital lasted not an hour, or two hours, but five days. The leaders tried to hold it back; the masses answered with increased pressure and marched forward. They had against them the old state, behind whose traditional façade a mighty power was still assumed to exist, the liberal bourgeoisie with the State Duma, the Land and City Unions, the military-industrial organizations, academies, universities, a highly developed press, and finally the two strong socialist parties who put up a patriotic resistance to the assault from below. In the party of the Bolsheviks the insurrection had its nearest organization, but a headless organization with a

---

[2] In the late 19th century Russian intellectuals developed an agrarian socialist philosophy which placed great weight upon the importance of the peasant and his institutions and upon the moral duty of the intellectual to help the peasants improve their lives. This *narodnik* (populist) philosophy gave rise to a series of important revolutionary movements in the 19th century and served as a basis for the new party of Socialist Revolutionaries in the 20th century. Contrary to Trotsky's assertion here, Kerensky was a member of the Socialist Revolutionary party. [Editor's note]

scattered staff and with weak illegal nuclei. And nevertheless the revolution, which nobody in those days was expecting, unfolded, and just when it seemed from above as though the movement was already dying down, with an abrupt revival, a mighty convulsion, it seized the victory.

Whence came this unexampled force of aggression and self-restraint? It is not enough to refer to bitter feelings. Bitterness alone is little. The Petersburg workers, no matter how diluted during the war years with human raw material, had in their past a great revolutionary experience. In their aggression and self-restraint, in the absence of leadership and in the face of opposition from above, was revealed a vitally wellfounded, although not always expressed, estimate of forces and a strategic calculation of their own.

On the eve of the war the revolutionary layers of the workers had been following the Bolsheviks, and leading the masses after them. With the beginning of the war the situation had sharply changed: conservative groups lifted their heads, dragging after them a considerable part of the class. The revolutionary elements found themselves isolated, and quieted down. In the course of the war the situation began to change, at first slowly, but after the defeats faster and more radically. An active discontent seized the whole working class. To be sure, it was to an extent patriotically colored, but it had nothing in common with the calculating and cowardly patriotism of the possessing classes, who were postponing all domestic questions until after the victory. The war itself, its victims, its horror, its shame, brought not only the old, but also the new layers of workers into conflict with the tzarist régime. It did this with a new incisiveness and led them to the conclusion: we can no longer endure it. The conclusion was universal; it welded the masses together and gave them a mighty dynamic force.

The army had swollen, drawing into itself millions of workers and peasants. Every individual had his own people among the troops: a son, a husband, a brother, a relative. The army was no longer insulated, as before the war, from the people. One met with soldiers now far oftener; saw them off to the front, lived with them when they came home on leave, chatted with them on the streets and in the tramways about the front, visited them in the hospitals. The workers' districts, the barracks, the front, and to an extent the villages too, became communicating vessels. The workers would know what the soldiers were thinking and feeling. They had innumerable conversations about the war, about the people who were getting rich out of the war, about the generals, government, tzar and tzarina. The soldier would say about the war: To hell with it! And the worker would answer about the government: To hell with it! The soldier would say: Why then do you sit still here in the center? The worker would answer: We can't do anything with bare hands; we stubbed our toe against the army in 1905. The soldier would reflect: What if we should all start at once! The worker: That's it, all at once! Conversations of this kind before the war were conspirative and carried on by two's; now they were going on everywhere, on every occasion, and almost openly, at least in the workers' districts.

The tzar's intelligence service every once in a while took its soundings very successfully. Two weeks before the revolution a spy, who signed himself with the name Krestianinov, reported a conversation in a tramcar traversing the workers' suburb. The soldier was telling how in his regiment eight men were under hard labor because last autumn they refused to shoot at the workers of the Nobel factory, but shot at the police instead. The conversation went on quite openly, since in the workers' districts the police and the spies preferred to remain unnoticed. "'We'll get even with them,' the soldier concluded." The report reads further: "A skilled worker answered him: 'For that it is necessary to organize so that all will be like one.' The soldier answered: 'Don't you worry, we've been organized a long time. . . . They've drunk enough blood. Men are suffering in the trenches and here they are fattening their bellies!' . . . No special disturbance occurred. February 10, 1917. Krestianinov." Incomparable spy's epic. "No special disturbance occurred." They will occur, and that soon: this tramway conversation signalizes their inexorable approach.

The spontaneousness of the insurrection Mstislavsky illustrates with a curious example: When the "Union of Officers of February 27," formed just after the revolution, tried to determine with a questionnaire who first led out the Volynsky regiment, they received seven answers naming seven initiators of this decisive action. It is very likely, we may add, that a part of the initiative really did belong to several soldiers, nor is it impossible that the chief initiator fell in the street fighting, carrying his name with him into oblivion. But that does not diminish the historic importance of his nameless initiative. Still more important is another side of the matter which will carry us beyond the walls of the barrack room. The insurrection of the battalions of the Guard, flaring up a complete surprise to the liberal and legal socialist circles, was no surprise at all to the workers. Without the insurrection of the workers the Volynsky regiment would not have gone into the street. That street encounter of the workers with the Cossacks, which a lawyer observed from his window and which he communicated by telephone to the deputy, was to them both an episode in an impersonal process: a factory locust stumbled against a locust from the barracks. But it did not seem that way to the Cossack who had dared wink to the worker, nor to the worker who instantly decided that the Cossack had "winked in a friendly manner." The molecular interpenetration of the army with the people was going on continuously. The workers watched the temperature of the army and instantly sensed its approach to the critical mark. Exactly this was what gave such inconquerable force to the assault of the masses, confident of victory.

Here we must introduce the pointed remark of a liberal official trying to summarize his February observations: "It is customary to say that the movement began spontaneously, the soldiers themselves went into the street. I cannot at all agree with this. After all, what does the word 'spontaneously' mean? . . . Spontaneous conception is still more out of place in sociology than in natural science. Owing to the fact that none of the revolutionary leaders with a name was able to hang his label on the movement, it becomes not impersonal but merely nameless." This formulation of the question, incomparably more serious than Miliukov's references to German agents and Russian spontaneousness, belongs to a former Procuror who met the revolution in the position of a tzarist senator. It is quite possible that his experience in the courts permitted Zavadsky to realize that a revolutionary insurrection cannot arise either at the command of foreign agents, or in the manner of an impersonal process of nature.

The same author relates two incidents which permitted him to look as through a keyhole into the laboratory of the revolutionary process. On Friday, February 24, when nobody in the upper circles as yet expected a revolution in the near future, a tramcar in which the senator was riding turned off quite unexpectedly, with such a jar that the windows rattled and one was broken, from the Liteiny into a side street, and there stopped. The conductor told everybody to get off: "The car isn't going any farther." The passengers objected, scolded, but got off. "I can still see the face of that unanswering conductor: angrily resolute, a sort of wolf look." The movement of the tramways stopped everywhere as far as the eye could see. That resolute conductor, in whom the liberal official could already catch a glimpse of the "wolf look," must have been dominated by a high sense of duty in order all by himself to stop a car containing officials on the streets of imperial Petersburg in time of war. It was just such conductors who stopped the car of the monarchy and with practically the same words — this car does not go any farther! — and who ushered out the bureaucracy, making no distinction in the rush of business between a general of gendarmes and a liberal senator. The conductor on the Liteiny boulevard was a conscious factor of history. It had been necessary to educate him in advance.

During the burning of the District Court a liberal jurist from the circle of that same senator started to express in the street his regret that a roomful of judicial decisions and notarial archives was perishing. An elderly man of somber aspect dressed as a worker angrily objected: "We will be able to divide the houses and the lands ourselves, and without your archives." Probably the episode is rounded out in a literary manner. But there were plenty of elderly workers like that in the crowd, capable of making the necessary retort. They themselves had nothing to do with burning the District Court: why burn it? But at least you could not frighten them with "excesses" of this kind. They were arming the masses with the necessary ideas not only against the tzarist police, but against liberal jurists who feared most of all lest there should burn up in the fire of the revolution the notarial deeds of property. Those nameless, austere statesmen of the factory and streets did not fall out of the sky: they had to be educated.

In registering the events of the last days of February the Secret Service also remarked that the movement was "spontaneous," that is, had no planned leadership from above; but they immediately added: "with the generally propagandized condition of the proletariat." This appraisal hits the bull's-eye: the professionals of the struggle with the revolution, before entering the cells vacated by the revolutionists, took a much closer view of what was happening than the leaders of liberalism.

The mystic doctrine of spontaneousness explains nothing. In order correctly to appraise the situation and determine the moment for a blow at the enemy, it was necessary that the masses or their guiding layers should make their examination of historical events and have their criteria for estimating them. In other words, it was necessary that there should be not masses in the abstract, but masses of Petrograd workers and Russian workers in general, who had passed through the revolution of 1905, through the Moscow insurrection of December 1905, shattered against the Semenovsky Regiment of the Guard. It was necessary that throughout this mass should be scattered workers who had thought over the experience of 1905, criticized the constitutional illusions of the liberals and Mensheviks, assimilated the perspectives of the revolution, meditated hundreds of times about the question of the army, watched attentively what was going on in its midst — workers capable of making revolutionary inferences from what they observed and communicating them to others. And finally, it was necessary that there should be in the troops of the garrison itself progressive soldiers, seized, or at least touched, in the past by revolutionary propaganda.

In every factory, in each guild, in each company, in each tavern, in the military hospital, at the transfer stations, even in the depopulated villages, the molecular work of revolutionary thought was in progress. Everywhere were to be found the interpreters of events, chiefly from among the workers, from whom one inquired, "What's the news?" and from whom one awaited the needed words. These leaders had often been left to themselves, had nourished themselves upon fragments of revolutionary generalizations arriving in their hands by various routes, had studied out by themselves between the lines of the liberal papers what they needed. Their class instinct was refined by a political criterion, and though they did not think all their ideas through to the end, nevertheless their thought ceaselessly and stubbornly worked its way in a single direction. Elements of experience, criticism, initiative, self-sacrifice, seeped down through the mass and created, invisibly to a superficial glance but no less decisively, an inner mechanics of the revolutionary movement as a conscious process. To the smug politicians of liberalism and tamed socialism everything that happens among masses is customarily represented as an instinctive process, no matter whether they are dealing with an anthill or a beehive. In reality the thought which was drilling through the thick of the working class was far bolder, more penetrating, more conscious, than those little ideas by which the educated classes live. Moreover, this thought was more scientific: not only because it was to a considerable degree fertilized with the methods of Marxism, but still more because it was ever nourishing itself on the living experience of the masses which were soon to take their place on the revolutionary arena. Thoughts are scientific if they correspond to an objective process and make it possible to influence that process and guide it. Were these qualities possessed in the slightest degree by the ideas of those government circles who were inspired by the Apocalypse and believed in the dreams of Rasputin? Or maybe the ideas of the liberals were scientifically grounded, who hoped that a backward Russia, having joined the scrimmage of the capitalist giants, might win at one and the same time victory and parliamentarism? Or maybe the intellectual life of those circles of the intelligentsia was scientific, who slavishly adapted themselves to this liberalism, senile since childhood, protecting their imaginary independence the while with long-dead metaphors? In truth here

was a kingdom of spiritual inertness, specters, superstition and fictions, a kingdom, if you will, of "spontaneousness." But have we not in that case a right to turn this liberal philosophy of the February revolution exactly upside down? Yes, we have a right to say: At the same time that the official society, all that many-storied superstructure of ruling classes, layers, groups, parties and cliques, lived from day to day by inertia and automatism, nourishing themselves with the relics of worn-out ideas, deaf to the inexorable demands of evolution, flattering themselves with phantoms and foreseeing nothing — at the same time, in the working masses there was taking place an independent and deep process of growth, not only of hatred for the rulers, but of critical understanding of their impotence, an accumulation of experience and creative consciousness which the revolutionary insurrection and its victory only completed.

To the question, Who led the February revolution? we can then answer definitely enough: Conscious and tempered workers educated for the most part by the party of Lenin. But we must here immediately add: This leadership proved sufficient to guarantee the victory of the insurrection, but it was not adequate to transfer immediately into the hands of the proletarian vanguard the leadership of the revolution.

FROM MARCH TO OCTOBER: WHY DID RUSSIA SEEK EVER MORE RADICAL SOLUTIONS?

Russia Faced a Foreign Policy Dilemma

VICTOR CHERNOV

Victor Chernov (1873–1952), the leader and chief theorist of the Socialist Revolutionary party, was born at Saratov on the lower Volga. His grandfather had been a serf, and Chernov's life was deeply influenced by his own lasting concern with agrarian problems. In 1917 he served as Minister of Agriculture in the Provisional Government from May through August 26. Here Chernov describes the Provisional Government's efforts to devise a foreign policy that would be acceptable both to its own members and to the Petrograd Soviet of Workers' and Soldiers' Deputies.

I N his *Days* Shulgin tells how Kerensky, during the street disturbances of February, 1917, burst into the room of the Provisional Committee of the Imperial Duma, handed them a folio of papers saying, "Hide them! They are the secret treaties with our Allies!" and hastened off. In all the turmoil there was no place to hide the state secret contained in that folio; it had to be concealed beneath the table with its long hanging cloth, in the same room. What unconscious symbolism!

The confused heritage of old Tsarist diplomacy, burdened with overdrawn notes, and now bequeathed to the new Russia, was hastily hidden under the table. These secret treaties had been concluded by the Allies in various combinations and without each other's knowledge. Identical territorial acquisitions had been promised simultaneously to different Allies. At Versailles the victorious Allies later found it a long and difficult task to untangle this confusion.

The new Russia did not know what to do with this diplomatic inheritance. Its weight would cut its shoulders and burden its democratic conscience.

Bolshevism advanced the abrupt revolutionary demand: publish these documents immediately, and thus deal a moral blow to the World War. The Cadets, led by Miliukov, were at the opposite political pole: an heir, in accepting the legator's property, also accepts his financial obligations, and all his rights of suit, so new Russia was bound unconditionally by the secret treaties, and must not depart from them. United Soviet democracy, led by the bloc of Social Revolutionaries and Social Democrats, could follow neither Lenin nor Miliukov.[1]

[1] Chernov is principally concerned in these pages with the struggle between (1) the Provisional

From Victor Chernov, *The Great Russian Revolution* (New Haven, 1936), pp. 193–207. Reprinted by permission of the Yale University Press.

39

The one-sided publication of the secret documents of the Entente prior to the end of the war or the German Revolution, which would simultaneously expose the secrets of Wilhelm's diplomacy, it regarded as a blow, not at the war as such, but only at one warring side. It meant disrupting the Entente from within, and consciously or unconsciously abetting Hohenzollern Germany.

But Soviet democracy considered it absolutely necessary to break through the web in which the Allies had entangled themselves by the initiative of Tsarist diplomacy. From this viewpoint new Russia was morally entitled to postpone till after the war the exposure of all the filth, the unceremonious greed, the saturnalia of predatory appetites, expressed in the secret treaties, but only on condition of immediate annulment of their binding force. Of all the inter-Allied treaties it left only one in effect: the obligation to end the war by a general peace, not by an egoistic, separate withdrawal from the World War. From now on the new Russian diplomacy must strive to elaborate a positive, concrete program of universal democratic peace, a peace without victors or vanquished, a peace which would not leave behind either chauvinist triumph or insatiable thirst for revenge.

Miliukov could not carry out this policy. From the outbreak of the war he had staked everything on the country's patriotic enthusiasm. He had cleverly turned it against the yearning for a separate peace, which, luckily for him, had been associated with the

program of Rasputin's reactionary clique. He had regarded the alliance with England and France as a promise of Russia's future imitation of them in domestic reconstruction. Earlier, during the Balkan War, he had given new life to the motifs of Neo-Slavism which were to undermine the Hapsburg Empire. He had formulated an extensive program of Russia's territorial acquisitions, including Constantinople, and the Bosphorus and Dardanelles, unification of Poland under the Russian scepter, including Posen, Cracow, Lwow, and Danzig, East Prussia as an additional Baltic province, Sub-Carpathian Russia and Bukovina, as Ukrainian lands, and the territories of Hither Asia which had once been Greater Armenia.

Military failures did not lead Miliukov to abandon these plans for conquest. Whatever Ally tipped the scales in favor of the Entente, the victory would be common, and then would be the time to present the old treaties. The new pacifist ideas did not move him from his accustomed track. "In all his speeches he emphasized vigorously the pacifist aims of the war for liberation, but always linked them closely with Russia's national duties and interests." An enduring peace required the destruction of the military power of the Central Empires, their forcible disarmament, and the "organization of Europe" by the victors. *Mutatis mutandis*, the German imperialists were as eager to be the "pacifiers" and "organizers of Europe," in accord with their "national duties and interests." Miliukov shrugged his shoulders at the idea that the socialist parties of the various countries could, during the war, agree on some general plan of democratic peace and then, by peaceful pressure or threat of revolution, break down the resistance of the warring governments. He was firmly convinced that only the Russians took this seriously. "The overwhelming majority of socialists of both warring groups has adopted the national viewpoint," and neither Zimmerwalds and Kienthals nor even Stockholm conferences could move

Government, which he also refers to as "censitary government"; and (2) the Petrograd Soviet of Workers' and Soldiers' Deputies. The Soviet, a self-appointed body which received wide support from workers and soldiers, exercised more real political authority inside the nation than did the Provisional Government and was in essence a second, unofficial government. To Chernov, the Soviet represents "United Soviet democracy," "Soviet democracy," and "revolutionary democracy." [Editor's note] them.[2] Still less could be said for their governments. Although with reluctance, he had to continue the policy of Tsarism: he carried on that policy because no other policy was possible, except a separate peace with Germany; i.e., a camouflaged alliance with victorious Germany. Later, when his card placed on the Entente was topped by the Bolsheviks, Miliukov went quite calmly to the zone of German occupation, to seek salvation in friendship with the enemy of yesterday: that same Miliukov who had not shrunk from casting on his socialist opponents the suspicion of Germanophilism, for which the crowd was then ready to stone to death.

Miliukov stood with both feet on the well-trodden path of the old Realpolitik. Its point of departure was the *sacro egoismo nazionale,* while its façade and signboard boasted of the "last" war, the war "of liberation," the war "to end war." Soviet democracy sought new paths in foreign policy. It tried to end the war, not by military fortune, but on a foundation of right. It broke with secret diplomacy. It tried to appeal to the peoples against the governments to strive for a juridical organization of all humanity, for the subjection of the jealous sovereignties of separate states to a supranational supersovereignty. It wanted what was then termed a mad Utopia, and has since made the career of able statesmen like Briand.

A collision was inevitable. Soviet democracy published its famous "appeal to the peoples of the world." It urged all peoples to make an honest and heroic effort to rally from the war hypnosis, to seek a peace without victors and vanquished, without one-sided dictation and helpless submission. It appealed particularly to the German

people, whose armies were menacing revolutionary Russia, to overthrow the empire of the Hohenzollerns, as the Russian people had the Romanovs, and then to take joint measures to stop the World War. Meanwhile, it declared its firm intention of defending by force of arms the boundaries of the Russian Revolution against the armies of German imperialism.

The Provisional Government took a step forward in publishing an appeal to its citizens. "The aim of free Russia is not to dominate other peoples, not to rob them of their national property, not to seize by force other peoples' territories, but to establish a firm peace, based on the self-determination of peoples. The Russian people does not strive to increase its power abroad at the expense of other peoples, nor does it aim to enslave or degrade." But the close of the appeal again mentioned the "full honoring of our obligations toward our Allies"; the specter of the secret treaties was again evoked, and the fine words of the appeal as a whole were called in question. Tsarist diplomacy, while placing its seal on the scandalous contents of the treaties with one hand, with the other had traced the words of the Tsar's first manifesto on the declaration of war: "God is our witness that, not for vain and worldly glory, not for violence and oppression have we taken up arms, but only to defend the Russian state."

Miliukov himself proves that the ambiguity of the appeal was no accident. Only "after yielding to the majority had he consented to publish the appeal on war aims." He purposely chose the least binding form, "not a diplomatic note, but an appeal to the citizens." He selected "expressions which would not preclude his former understanding of our foreign policy, and would not require him to make any changes in that policy." In other words, Miliukov merely consented to *pretend* to choose a new path. When Nekrasov tried to persuade the representatives of Soviet democracy "to interpret the evasive terms of the appeal as a concession by the government," Miliukov

[2] Reference is made here to conferences of the Second International (organization of socialists) at Zimmerwald (September, 1915) and Kienthal (April, 1916), both in Switzerland, and at Stockholm in 1917. At each conference the socialists of the nations involved tried unsuccessfully to take a firm stand against the war and to find ways of bringing peace. [Editor's note]

"reserved his right, in case the compromise should be interpreted in one-sided fashion, to explain it in his own sense, and to elucidate its vague terms in accord with his earlier policy."

The subtle, refined craft proper in dealing with a practiced diplomat is seldom helpful in dealing with a democracy of toilers. Russian *émigré* revolutionaries were now returning to Russia via England and Scandinavia, and in the Executive Committee Chernov soon made a report explaining that all the communiqués, interviews, etc., of the Russian Ministry of Foreign Affairs meant but one thing: the revolution had made absolutely no change in the foreign policy and war aims of Tsarist Russia; the agreements concluded by Tsarist diplomacy were still considered inviolable for revolutionary Russia; no one abroad had even heard of the proclamation on war aims, intended solely for home consumption. This was confirmed by the "representatives of Allied socialism" who came to Russia at that time. Some of them also represented their governments. Miliukov later accused them of "yielding more to the Soviet than was reconcilable with the common interests of the Allies and their own national interests."

As a matter of fact even Albert Thomas felt that the question of peace had been greatly complicated by Russia's claim to Constantinople and the Dardanelles. This had unleashed the appetites of other Allied countries, and nationalist currents seeking equivalent "compensation" had taken the upper hand. Thomas assumed that Russian renunciation of excessive demands would aid in securing a revision of war aims in other countries; for example, the plans of French chauvinists to seize the entire Rhineland and break up Germany. As a realistic politician, he felt that Germany would fight to the last man against such schemes, and that even if peace were made on such conditions, it would be but a brief interlude before a new war.

Having discussed the situation, the leaders of the Soviet resolved to try to get the Provisional Government to communicate officially to the Allies the contents of its proclamation on war aims in the form of a diplomatic document. They learned that Miliukov refused categorically, and in general declined to make any *démarche* to the Allies toward revising war aims and drawing up a publishable peace program; in other words, he refused to abandon secret diplomacy with its burden of secret treaties and to adopt open diplomacy under public control.

This refusal marked the beginning of a crisis in the government. A bitter political duel now began between Miliukov and Kerensky. The latter seemed to adopt the "Zimmerwald" position.

"Russian democracy is now master of the Russian land," he declared in conversation with the Frenchmen, Moutet, Cachin, Lafont, and the Englishmen, O'Grady, Sanders, and Thorne.

We have resolved once and for all to put a stop in our country to all attempts at imperialism and conquest. . . . The enthusiasm which fills Russian democracy does not flow from any partial ideas, not even from the idea of the fatherland, as old Europe has understood it, but from ideas which compel us to think that the dream of the brotherhood of the entire world will soon become a reality. . . . We expect you, in your countries, to exert on other classes the same decisive pressure that we here in Russia have exerted on our bourgeois classes, which have now proclaimed their renunciation of imperialist ambitions.

Kerensky did not fail to point out that he alone within the government represented revolutionary democracy. That was true, and untrue. He was the only minister who also held a responsible position (vice president) in the Soviet; but he did not formally "represent" any one in the government. On the other hand, he was not entirely "alone." Even in the question of the "fatherland vs. humanity," he had two faithful allies, Nekrasov and Tereshchenko. These two were a peculiar type of "internationalist," associated not with socialism but with Russian Masonry. The Slavophil Internationalist, Prince Lvov, and the Masonic Internationalists, Nekrasov and Teresh-chenko, supported the "all but Zimmer-waldian" Kerensky, and Miliukov had to capitulate, at least in form. The declaration on war aims was dispatched to the Allies as an official document. But even here the diplomat's resourceful mind found a way out: Miliukov added a preface identifying the declaration on war aims with the "lofty ideas" "constantly expressed by many out-standing leaders in the Allied countries." He declared that in Russia there was a "national striving" to carry the war "to a decisive conclusion," to obtain "sanctions and guarantees" (annexations and indem-nities?) which would make new wars im-possible. Finally, he once more promised to "fulfil Russia's obligations to the Allies."

The terms of the original proclamation, which Miliukov himself called "evasive," through this commentary were made more than ambiguous.

Miliukov's constant reference to Russia's obligations had already helped the Bol-sheviks pass resolutions at the biggest fac-tories in Petrograd (Triangle, Parviainen, etc.), demanding publication of the secret treaties, in order to examine Russia's obli-gations toward her Allies, and to discover whether their fulfilment was compatible with the democratic conscience of a revolu-tionary country. They were presented with another trump in their game.

The majority in the Soviet was literally astounded by Miliukov's note. It inclined to regard it as a deliberate stab in the back, a gesture of provocation, a challenge. In any case, it felt it had been deceived. In-stead of the promised communication to the Allies renouncing a policy of conquest, here was an attempt to dissolve the previous and not entirely satisfactory assurances in a sea of conventional diplomatic commonplaces.

Even the date of Miliukov's note seemed a mockery. It was dated April 18, Old Style, and this was May 1, New Style — the day on which the international holiday of labor and peace was traditionally cele-brated in Russia. On this day the streets of

Petrograd had witnessed big demonstra-tions, and the working class of Russia felt its might as never before.

The startled Executive Committee of the Soviet assembled on the night of April 19–20, and had not yet had time to discuss what had happened, when news came that the Finnish, Kuxholm and One Hundred and Eightieth Infantry and the Second Baltic Fleet were marching spontaneously from their barracks to the Marinsky Palace, to arrest the Provisional Government. In all working-class suburbs crowds were gathering to demonstrate in the center of the city. "Treason! Provocation!" No other words could describe the government's action.

Measures were immediately taken. Soviet delegations were sent to urge the soldiers and workers to refrain from action, since the Soviet undertook to liquidate the conflict with the government. Fortunately, the Marinsky Palace was empty. The military detachments which had collected, after tranquilizing speeches by the Soviet's orators, returned obediently to their bar-racks.

That evening the Provisional Govern-ment met with the Executive Committee of the Soviet. The members of the govern-ment read a series of reports on the country's grave, almost critical position, as if trying to create an impression that quarrels about the texts of the declarations were a mere bagatelle, in comparison with the impera-tive necessity for making every effort to avert imminent catastrophe, in which all conquests of the revolution would perish. With tremulous voice Guchkov described the tragedy of men of his type; compelled to choose between dynasty and fatherland, they had renounced their oath and joined the revolution, but now saw that this last, heroic remedy brought no salvation. Prince Lvov said that the government was not clinging to power; it was willing then and there to yield it to the leaders of the Soviet, if they thought they could cope better with the situation. The representatives of the Soviet became thoughtful: at bottom they felt an even greater repulsion for power and its responsibilities than before. Yet outwardly they held firm; the seriousness of the general situation increased the need for a logical and active foreign policy. Sukhanov spoke of the extreme danger to the new revolutionary Russia with each day that the war was prolonged beyond absolute necessity. Chernov criticized severely the entire activity of the Ministry of Foreign Affairs. While acknowledging the abilities of his political opponent, Miliukov, he concluded that the latter might be very useful, for example, as Minister of Education; as Minister of Foreign Affairs he would remain a source of weakness and discord in the government and the country, for by his public recognition of the Tsarist war aims, he had become absolutely unacceptable to the democracy of toilers. Tseretelli sought a formula to which the Provisional Government could agree without inward difficulty, in order to satisfy fully the aroused political conscience of the masses.

Finally, by the evening of April 21 it was agreed that the government would give an official explanation of two points in its note. On April 22 it explained that the reference to the national desire for "a decisive victory over the enemy" meant desire for the triumph of the idea of renunciation of conquest, while "sanctions and guarantees" meant, not one-sided punishment of the defeated (as originally understood in Soviet circles), but a system of international tribunals, limitation of armaments, and similar universal measures. The soviet majority considered it unnecessary to insist further or haggle over words. It was willing to facilitate the government's retreat. More important than any texts was Miliukov's defeat and the growing possibility of his retirement.

But late on the evening of April 20, when the Soviet "Centrists" had succeeded in calming working-class and military Petrograd, bourgeois Petrograd went down to the street, to give moral support to its minister, menaced by working-class democ-racy. Miliukov spoke to the demonstrators from his balcony. When he said that behind the shouts, "Down with Miliukov!" he seemed to hear "Down with Russia!" the bourgeois crowd burst into prolonged and noisy applause. It longed for the well-tried formula, "I am the State," the never-failing attribute of a "strong government." The bourgeoisie was soon to feel that from a civilian this formula was far less imposing than from a man on whose shoulders there quivered a general's epaulets.

The rumor of the bourgeois demonstration on the previous evening sufficed to re-arouse working-class Petrograd on April 21. The movement was begun by Vyborg district, where the Bolsheviks were especially strong. This time the Vyborg district acted in defiance even of the Central Committee of its own party. Its slogan was "Down with the Provisional Government!" It proposed to repeat the February days, and perhaps carry out a new overturn. Lenin and his staff considered this premature and rash, but they were helpless. The demonstrators could not be dissuaded even by a delegation from the Soviet, headed by its president Chkheidze.

Meanwhile new and alarming reports had come. Military detachments with artillery had again appeared on the Palace Square. This time they were led by the commander of the Petrograd district, General Kornilov. Other military detachments refused to obey him, and in great excitement were holding meetings, asking the Soviet what they should do. Civil war seemed about to break out again on the streets and squares of Petrograd. That evening clashes began between groups demonstrating for and against Miliukov and the Provisional Government. Shots rang out. The Red Guards of Vyborg district resolved to prove that the streets of Petrograd belonged to them, and not to the bourgeois "well-dressed public."

As always, each side blamed the other for the clash. Both suspected provocation by some third "sinister force." The Cadets talked of Germans backing the Bolsheviks, the Bolsheviks of monarchists backing the Cadets.

At this point the Soviet realized that the time had come, not for words, but for decisive action. Under its pressure General Kornilov had to rescind his orders. The artillery disappeared from the Palace Square. To avoid all attempts by the Right or Left to use armed force, all the barracks were informed that without a command of the Executive Committee, sealed with its seal and signed by specially named and empowered persons, no military detachment was to stir. The Executive Committee also forbade all street demonstrations for three days. The Soviet's automobiles dashed through the streets scattering these categorical commands; as if at the wave of a magic wand, everything became quiet.

Thus the Soviet acted as dictator, but only for a few hours, and only to forestall any further provocation to civil war. We know now that Kornilov, like Krymov, was indignant at the government's helplessness, and thirsted for the "ruthless mopping up of Petrograd." The Soviet robbed him of that chance. The strong-willed, ambitious general could not endure this affront. He handed in his resignation. The Provisional Government was entirely on his side, and was sincerely horrified to think that the Soviet had dared to encroach on his prerogatives. Once more it declared with indignation that the "power of the commander of the troops of the Petrograd military district remains in full force, and control of the troops may be exercised only by him." The Soviet did not argue. It did not want a dictatorship, and had merely exercised it at a critical moment since no one else could have done what had to be done. It then returned to its domestic affairs. It did not even pause to reflect that it had, in effect, usurped the rights of the district commander. Such had not been its intention; it was only the result of its effort to prevent a civil war. The government itself realized this; it mentioned in its proclamation that

the order of the Soviet "was evidently intended to forestall attempts of individual persons or groups to call out the troops." That was true, although even the district commander became just such an "individual" in the eyes of the Soviet when he aroused its suspicion because of his rash impulses, which might have touched off a civil war. But the Provisional Government as a whole also feared and did not want a civil war. It could be dissatisfied because someone else, and not it, had done what had been done. That was its real tragedy.

That which it could have suspected earlier now became clear to the government. Relations between it and the Soviet could easily be defined. On the one hand, formal power without real force, on the other actual strength without formal power. Powerless government, and governmentless force.

This divorce between governmental power and actual strength had to be ended as soon as possible. Such was the general conclusion. In particular, Miliukov, as Minister of Foreign Affairs, had become a great danger to the entire government.

Under other conditions all the authority lost by Miliukov would have been gained by Kerensky. But Kerensky had made a terrible blunder: the odious addition to the note was no surprise to him, as it was to the Soviet leaders. Kerensky "later tried to deny" that he had assented to this note; an official communiqué immediately explained that the "note of the Minister of Foreign Affairs had been carefully considered by the Provisional Government, and its text adopted *unanimously*." Kerensky's popularity, which had grown rapidly since the first days of revolution, tottered for the first time, and seemed on the verge of collapse. It was long before Kerensky could forgive Miliukov for that moment of weakness which he had to justify even to his most devoted friends. Sharp scenes occurred within the government. Kerensky presented his resignation. General Kornilov insisted on resigning. Guchkov's resignation seemed imminent. Least of all was said of the natural step; namely, Miliukov's resignation. A group was growing which demanded a resignation of the cabinet and a coalition with representatives of Soviet democracy. They caught up Chernov's idea of transferring Miliukov to the Ministry of Education.

Meanwhile Kerensky published a letter written for him by Chernov, explaining why revolutionary democracy had been ignored in forming the government and why he had entered the cabinet on his own risk. Noting the beginning of a new era — its responsible participation in governing the country — he concluded that revolutionary democracy, whether through the Soviet or the socialist parties, would delegate to the government its formal representatives who would report their activity to it; he promised that such would henceforth be his own rôle.

Soviet circles still hesitated as to whether or not to adopt such a novel line of conduct. At one session of the Executive Committee, participation in the government was rejected 23 to 22, with 8 abstentions. At the next meeting it was adopted 41 to 18, with 3 abstentions. When this decision had been adopted, it turned out that the censitary part of the government originally had in mind, not forming a genuine coalition government, but rather bringing into the cabinet, preferably for the newly established post of Minister of Labor, one more socialist, some labor leader, like Plekhanov, who by the historical popularity of his big name would reënforce the government's badly shaken authority and be a living shield against attacks from the Left. Negotiations dragged on and more than once seemed on the verge of complete fiasco, although efforts to arrange a coalition were made not only by Kerensky, Nekrasov, and Tereshchenko, but also by such a skillful diplomat as Albert Thomas. In Soviet circles a movement grew in favor of taking direct responsibility for the government's policy only on condition of real, numerical preponderance within the cabinet. The All-Russian Congress of Soviets of Peasants' Deputies, then in session, expressed this as a demand for a Soviet majority within the cabinet. In addition, the unsuccessful experiment in the provinces with Prince Lvov's commissars and instructions led them to demand with insistence that Internal Affairs be transferred to socialist hands. That would have been difficult without the retirement of Prince Lvov, a chief defender of the idea of reorganizing the government along coalition lines. There was much disagreement about Chernov; the crisis had broken out and the question of the coalition been decided in his absence. The Left wing of the Social Revolutionary party demanded that the Ministry of Foreign Affairs be transferred to him; the majority of the party considered that, as author of the program for "socialization of the land," he should take over the Ministry of Agriculture, in order to prepare the land reform. The Cadet party, unable to forgive his victorious campaign against Miliukov and his participation in the international conference at Zimmerwald, objected to his participation in the government. Finally, Chernov, summoned from Moscow by telegraph, protested against exchanging a Soviet for a government post; he conditioned his assent, first, on participation of the Social Democratic leader, Tseretelli, in the government, and, second, on the transfer of the Ministry of Supply, so closely connected with agriculture, to some socialist; but the Cadet Shingarev clung to this post. Kerensky, who but recently "had dreamed of raising justice in Russia to an unprecedented height," had turned cold, and thirsted to replace Guchkov. He was now dreaming of placing the revolutionary army "on an unprecedented height," and crowning it with laurels of victory. To reconcile all these difficulties was like "squaring the circle." . . .

A Demoralized Army Spread Dissatisfaction among the People

NICHOLAS N. GOLOVINE

Before the revolution Lieutenant General Nicholas N. Golovine was a Professor in the Russian Imperial General Staff College and Chief of Staff of the Russian Armies on the Rumanian Front. He is recognized as the best Russian authority on the history of the World War. His studies on the Russian Army, pursued diligently for many years after his emigration from Russia, are deeply affected by a strong interest in the sociological impact of the war and the revolution upon Russia's soldiers. In the section presented here, the relationship between the army and the people of the nation is drawn very clearly.

As one studies the attitude of the bulk of the troops in the first days of the Revolution, it becomes obvious that the degree of revolutionary feeling, and the tendency to yield to demoralizing influences increased proportionately with the distance from the front. This was observable throughout the entire year. The fact that every new wave of disintegration came from the rear was based on that; and the process of collapse in the army illustrated a kind of general psychological law. General Serrigny . . . noticed the same thing in the French theater of war. He writes:

This development made itself clear during the defeatist propaganda of 1917. Regiments which had been relieved from service at the front, and were resting in the rear, were the first to yield to such propaganda; and they were infected with the poison by reinforcement units and by men who had been on home leave. Germany experienced the same thing in October, 1918. She was in a state of complete disintegration. Her rear units and depot regiments were hoisting red flags and tearing the shoulder-straps from their officers, while troops in the firing line continued to fight gallantly. The latter, after the signing of the armistice, retreated across the Rhine in perfect order, and helped to restore it at home, for they had had no time to be infected. . . .

In Russia, the process of the spread of military disintegration from the rear to the front showed itself in another way. For in the northern front, behind which was the chief center of revolution, Petrograd, it developed more rapidly than elsewhere. Next came the western front, behind which lay the second focus of revolution, Moscow. The southwestern front, in the rear of which was Kiev, was in a more healthy state; and the waves of dissolution reached it only later on. . . . As for the armies on the Rumanian front, they made the best showing. They were on foreign soil, and that delayed the revolutionary process.

The Petrograd garrison, consisting of depot units, turned out to be the Revolution's driving force. Indeed it was its revolt that gave the Revolution its instant victory. The Baltic fleet and the fortress troops of Kronstadt, which were nearest to Petrograd, proved to be no less demoralized.

* * *

REPORTS OF THE MEMBERS OF THE DUMA

At least some approximate idea of the

From Nicholas N. Golovine, *The Russian Army in the World War* (New Haven, 1931), pp. 249–50, 252–56, 257–60, 272–74. Reprinted by permission of the Yale University Press.

47

attitude of the soldiers in the first month of the Revolution can be given by a report made by N. O. Yanushkevich, a member of the Duma, who, with other members, visited various sections of the front. His report was read before the Provisional Committee of the Duma, which in the first month of the Revolution sought to maintain control over the Provisional Government headed by Prince Lvov.

This report by Yanushkevich is typical. It is almost identical with the reports of other members of the Duma, who, in March, 1917, had been sent by the Provisional Government to visit the army. Undoubtedly, their common mission accounted for the similarity of their reports; and the mission they had been given was that of strengthening the army's faith in the Provisional Government. In their desire to win the confidence of the rank and file they risked seeming to play the part of demagogues. In Yanushkevich's report this may be seen in his tendency to find an explanation for all rank and file disorders in the "tactlessness" of officers not in sympathy with the Revolution. The following detail is characteristic: the committees are called in the report "soldiers' and officers' committees," the word "soldiers'" being placed before the word "officers'." Similar details, written with intent to please the soldier in general, may be found in many other places. But, broadly speaking, one must admit that all such envoys of the Provisional Government were filled with a profound, patriotic, and sincere desire to help the army through the impending crisis.

The Yanushkevich report offers added evidence of the social and psychological law already spoken of, namely, that the disintegration of an army begins in its rear. Yanushkevich states that the spirit of the troops grew better as one neared the front, and that the attitude of the men in the firing line was "so cheerful, joyous, and good that one felt reassured." "The soldiers," he said, "are waiting for something. . . ." That "waiting attitude" of the bulk of the troops in the first days following the collapse of the old *régime* has been noted by all observers. It is very significant from the psychological standpoint. Up to then the great majority of people had been wont to look passively upon all high questions of national importance; there everything was decided by the Tsar and his Government: and such an attitude was the product of centuries of habit. Now, and suddenly, everything was overturned. The newspapers, in which the soldiers now were greatly interested, the speakers to whom they now listened for hours, exhorted freedom; and, they said, the people were henceforward to decide everything for themselves. Most soldiers were still bewildered and did not know what to do. From somewhere deep down in their inner consciousness selfish desires would often arise: to take away the land from the landlords, to rob the *bourgeois*, to abandon the front, and go home. . . . But the fact that a lawful Government, although its authority was shaken, was still in existence tended to restrain such anarchistic tendencies, and, for a while, they remained subconscious. Under such conditions, the sounder elements at the front were inclined to rely upon the Duma and the Provisional Government. The ovations to the member of the Duma which Yanushkevich describes in his report were sincere. Few knew as yet that the Provisional Government had already been out-trumped by the Petrograd Soviet of Workers' and Soldiers' Deputies. However, the extreme revolutionary elements in the army already suspected it. This may be seen from this sentence in the Yanushkevich report: "We were also requested to let them send their representatives to Petrograd to learn what was going on there." Later on, such representatives were sent by every army. In this way those who advocated making the Revolution more radical were able to establish contact with the Petrograd Soviet, which aspired at the leadership of the whole revolutionary movement.

This, however, Yanushkevich failed to see. Strongly impressed by the outward side of his reception, he forgot completely that all crowd manifestations are always highly emotional and subject to change, and that mere appearances could not serve as a guaranty that the same crowd, within the shortest time, would not acclaim with equal enthusiasm something entirely different. Nor did he realize that the underlying causes of the split between the officers and their men were of a more serious nature than the alleged "tactlessness" of the former. That split marked the beginning of the hostility which eventually led to civil war. He likewise failed to understand that what was said about leaves of absence and the requests of the older soldiers to be sent home were ways of showing their unwillingness to go on fighting. That "refusal to wage war" was still confined to the subconscious in the case of most of the men; though they did not dare as yet to express it openly, it existed as a potential factor.

To show that our analysis is correct we shall cite the report of two members of the Duma, M. Maslennikov and M. Shmakov, who visited the southwestern front one month later in April. Heretofore, what had been taking place in the army at the time of Yanushkevich's visit appeared only in symptoms that were sporadic and barely perceptible, but everything had now become very plain. Moreover, it should be borne in mind that the disintegration of the southwestern front, visited by Maslennikov, proceeded at a slower pace than the northern, with Petrograd in its immediate rear.

As we consider the report of Maslennikov and Shmakov, the following fact must not be left out of sight: during the first month of the Revolution, the soldiers' soviets were being formed in every section of the front. The commanding officers, anxious to get control over that elemental movement in the rank and file, decided to create committees of men and to place representatives of the officers on those committees. They hoped that in that way the soldier's confidence in his officers might be restored, and the gap between them bridged anew. Instructions to take such action were given by

General Alexeev, who, as we have said, had replaced the Grand Duke as Commander-in-Chief.

By the time Maslennikov and Shmakov arrived at the front, committees in every regiment, division, and army corps had already been formed. Therefore, the task of the two members of the Duma, in so far as their being able to arrive at the attitude of the soldiers was concerned, was easier than that of Yanushkevich, who had visited the front when the committees were in process of formation and soldiers' meetings differed but little from casual gatherings apt to be carried away by the appeal of an eloquent speaker.

During their first visit to two regiments, described by Maslennikov and Shmakov as quite capable of fighting, they heard the formula "peace without annexations and contributions," which was the first slogan used by the defeatist propaganda of the Bolsheviks. The peculiar way in which the soldiers interpreted it may be judged from the many cases where they refused to dig new trenches, even at short distances in advance of their lines, and when trenches were needed to strengthen the positions they were holding.

A frank explanation of the meaning of "without annexations and contributions," as understood by the soldiers, was given to the members of the Duma by the chairman of a conference of the committees of the Second Army, a war-time lieutenant, whose manner of speech "was clearly Bolshevik." After he had described the Duma as representing the interests of the *bourgeois* classes and the capitalists, "he declared that the army would fight to the end only on the condition that the actual intentions of the Allies were made known, and Russia given a guaranty that the War was not being waged for their capitalistic aims. Taken as a whole, the speech gave the impression of being made to undermine the prestige of the Duma and the Provisional Government, as well as confidence in the Allies. It was with this situation that the Duma's representatives were, for the first time, confronted. The speech of the chairman had an enormous success. . . ." Further confirmation came when they visited the engineers of the Guard.

The political views of the presiding body of the committee [says the report] proved to be very radical, and Bolshevik in their nature. At this meeting the question of peace was taken up for the first time in our tour of the front. A member of the presiding body, the editor of a Lettish paper, suggested a peace conference as the quickest way to liquidate the War. Other speakers demanded that our agreements with the Allies be published, to show that we were not fighting for their imperialistic and capitalistic aims. A lack of confidence in our Allies was clearly felt. Not a single word was said that was hostile to Germany. Nevertheless, the meeting ended with cheers.

But, later on, Maslennikov and Shmakov encountered frank displays of defeatism:

Soldiers of infantry regiments have often cut the telephone wires from artillery "observers" to the batteries. They have threatened to lift the artillery men on their bayonets if the latter opened fire on the enemy. The same threat to use the bayonet prevents all machine-gun fire. Fraternizing is in progress, though not to the same extent as at Easter when it took a monstrous form. . . . We were told that in our trenches, some thirty yards from those of the Germans, the machine-guns were kept in their covers. . . .

*   *   *

THE RÔLE OF KERENSKY

The great majority of the soldiers, as we have said, had been bewildered, in the first days of the Revolution, by the rapidity and ease of the overthrow of the Imperial *régime*. Correspondingly and with bursts of excitement then, they acclaimed the new authority represented by the Provisional Government. But very soon news began to reach them that the actual power was not with that Government, but in the hands of the Petrograd Soviet of Workers' and Soldiers' Deputies. While the soldiers did not wish to break with the Provisional Government, carried to the top by the first

wave of the Revolution, their sympathies were with the Soviet organization. Highly significant is that part of the report which says that the views of the committees of those army units whose readiness to fight had been least impaired, were identical with the political views of the right wing of the Petrograd Soviet of Workers' and Soldiers' Deputies. That was true everywhere. M. Yakovlev proves it when he states that "in the first days of the Revolution these [military] committees were headed by Social-Revolutionist and Menshevist elements which tried to stretch the Revolution on the Procrustean bed of bourgeois half-reforms." Such forces were responsible for that tremendous popularity which Kerensky enjoyed among the soldiers at the front, from the beginning of the Revolution. Due to that popularity, in July he was made head of the Government, despite the fact that he no longer satisfied the revolutionary aims of the Petrograd Soviet. In this lay the tragedy in the rôle played by Kerensky. All his power depended on the support of soldiers at the front. And, while their attitude was being changed more slowly than was the mood of the Petrograd Soviet, that chief center of the Revolution, every further intensification of it tended to undermine Kerensky's strength and increase that of the Soviet. Under such circumstances the army, at the front, became an arena for the struggle between two tendencies. One aimed to keep the Revolution to politics alone, the other sought to change it, most speedily, into a social revolution. There is no doubt, however, that the representatives of the former, including Kerensky, were involuntarily pushing it on to transformation to the social phase. At the soldiers' meetings, Kerensky used to cry out, "Comrades, let us intensify the Revolution." Yet in that, as in similar cases, his words were dictated purely by demagoguery; and by means of it, he and his political sympathizers were seeking to gain power over the masses. The same foolish demagoguery also accounts for the orders given by Kerensky which led to the decline of the prestige of army leaders, to the destruction of discipline, and to further disintegration of the army. Kerensky did not understand what had been at work in the army from the beginning of the Revolution. There was another important factor in the situation. Though suffering from a psychosis, the troops had to go on fighting. It is only natural that the burden of the War — so little understood by them — which had weighed upon them for three years, had stirred in them a spirit of ever growing discontent and unwillingness. Consequently, from the beginning of the Revolution a desire to end the War, along with the political, economic, and social stimuli at work in every revolution, spread rapidly in both the army and the people.

DESERTERS

The vast increase in the number of cases of desertion and evasion of military service, which followed upon the outbreak of the Revolution, bears testimony to the urgent desire of the bulk of our soldiers to end the War. Let us go back to a few figures given in earlier chapters. The average monthly total of the sick increased 120 per cent, although the army suffered from no epidemic diseases and the sanitary conditions were no worse than before. The monthly record of deserters increased 400 per cent. Furthermore, beginning with March, 1917, there was a great "leakage" of soldiers from the front; and, in the rear, it became increasingly frequent for men to refuse, under varying pretexts, to join their regiments.

In the memoirs of General Polovtsev, who commanded the troops of the Petrograd military district, we find a description of one of the methods of desertion, and one practiced under the very nose of the Provisional Government.

A rumor [he says] to the effect that all soldiers over forty were to be discharged had got abroad, and an agitation began to make this rumor a reality. As a result, soldiers of forty commenced to desert, and to arrive in the capital with requests for legal discharges. They camped on the Semenovsky drill grounds, formed companies, founded their own republic, and sent deputations everywhere. Having no success, they commenced to parade the city, sometimes more than fifty companies at once. Chernov had encouraged them. Kerensky became enraged and had them driven out. I decided to starve them, and ordered their rations to be stopped. But it turned out that their republic could subsist independently, that they could live on what they made from the sale of cigarettes, from carrying baggage at the railroad stations, and the like.

. . . more than 2,000,000 men left the army in 1917 wilfully, and under various pretexts, since the Revolution began. It was a stupendous flow of men to the rear, that could only be called a spontaneous [de]-mobilization.

The above figures fully justify the statement that "the refusal to wage war" became, soon after the Revolution had begun, a part of its fundamental character. The political leaders, placed at the helm by the first changes, leaders who for the most part belonged to the progressive *bourgeoisie*, failed to understand it. Nor was it understood by Kerensky, who in July had succeeded Prince Lvov, and, assisted by the Social-Revolutionists of the Right, had become the master of Russia's destiny. They all continued to exhort the people to go on with the War until final victory was won.

Only one small group, the Bolsheviks headed by Lenin, staked their success by going to the army and calling for the immediate ending of the War.

*   *   *

THE OFFENSIVE OF JUNE, 1917

The main attack in the summer campaign of 1917 was to be launched by the southwestern front in the direction of Lemberg. The attacks on the northern, western, and Rumanian fronts were to be only of a subsidiary nature. On June 18, the Eleventh and the Seventh Armies began the offensive. An excellent plan had been worked out. Artillery and technical equipment in quantities previously unknown to Russia's forces were concentrated to prepare the infantry assault. All enemy works were literally leveled with the ground. Then and only then did the infantry advance in the zone of the enemy's fire; for the most part the picked shock units headed the advance. But the rest of the infantry followed with reluctance. Some regiments, having reached the enemy's lines, turned back on the pretext that the trenches had been so completely destroyed that it would be impossible to occupy them overnight. Nevertheless, thanks to the excellent artillery preparation and the heroic action of the picked units, the enemy positions were taken in the first two days. After that the Eleventh and Seventh Armies only marked time, inasmuch as the infantry was unwilling to advance further.

I feel in duty bound to report [wrote the commander of the Eleventh Army] that, despite the victory won on June 18 and 19 which should have strengthened the spirit and increased the zeal of the troops, no such effect could be seen in most regiments, while in some the conviction prevails that they have done their work and must go no further.

In the meantime, on June 23, the Eighth Army, on the left flank of the southwestern front, went into action. General Kornilov, commanding, had concentrated all his best units for a break through. But the same thing happened. The attack was successful, and even more so than in the center; for the Austro-Hungarian divisions facing the Eighth Army were of inferior quality. On the first day 7,000 prisoners and 48 guns were taken, and the Russian troops penetrated far into the enemy zone. But, as the advance progressed, the picked units, having suffered heavy losses, melted away, while the remaining infantry in their rear became so disorganized that a slight center attack from the enemy caused the entire army to fall back in the greatest confusion.

By July 2 this offensive on the southwestern front was at an end. The losses in the three armies amounted to 1,222 officers and 37,500 men. Such figures, compared

with the losses before the Revolution, were small. But they were suffered solely by the picked units and the few regiments not yet in disintegration. Thus they were heavy indeed, for they meant the loss of all elements imbued with a sense of duty, and available for preserving some sort of order among the troops. As they no longer existed, the three armies became nothing but tumultuous crowds, which any first pressure by the enemy could put to flight. Such pressure was brought to bear on the left flank of the Eleventh Army where at that time there had been concentrated 7 army corps or 20 divisions — a total of 240 battalions, 40 squadrons, 100 heavy and 475 field guns and howitzers. The opposing enemy had only 9 divisions, or some 83 battalions, with about 60 heavy and 400 field guns and howitzers. Despite such enormous numerical superiority, the detachments of the Eleventh Army began to retreat of their own accord. Soon the whole army was following in a panic. And the rest of the story may show how completely unfit it was to fight. On July 9 it reached the line of the Seret. An attack by three German companies put to flight the One Hundred and Twenty-sixth and the Second Finnish Divisions. Resistance to the advancing enemy was offered only by cavalry and infantry officers and non-commissioned officers supported by single soldiers. The rest of the infantry was fleeing, while crowds of deserters blocked every road. To tell how many there were it is enough to say that 12,000 were arrested in the neighborhood of Volochisk by a single battalion of picked men, who had been posted in the rear. And these fleeing mobs committed every act of violence. They murdered officers, robbed the people, and assaulted women and children.

On July 9 the committees and commissars of the Eleventh Army sent the Provisional Government the following telegram:

The German offensive, which began on our front on July 6, is turning into an immense catastrophe which perhaps threatens revolutionary Russia with ruin. A sudden and disasous change occurred in the attitude of the troops, who had recently advanced under the heroic leadership of a few units. Their zeal soon spent itself. The majority are in a state of growing disintegration. Authority and obedience exist no longer. Persuasion and admonition produce no effect. Threats and sometimes shots are the answer. . . . For hundreds of miles one can see lines of deserters, armed and unarmed, in good health and in high spirits, certain they will not be punished. The situation calls for strong measures. . . . An order to fire upon them was issued today by the Commander-in-Chief, with the approval of the commissars and committees. And all Russia should be told the truth. . . . Though she shudder at it, it will give her the necessary determination to deal with those who by their cowardice are ruining and betraying both their country and the Revolution.

A Primitive Peasants' War Gained Momentum

DAVID MITRANY

David Mitrany was born in Bucharest in 1888 and completed his advanced studies at London. He was once a member of the editorial staff of the *Manchester Guardian,* and has held teaching positions at London, Harvard, Yale, and Smith College. He has also been associated with the Royal Institute of International Affairs and is a Permanent Member of the Institute for Advanced Study at Princeton. Mitrany has long been interested in the special characteristics of the peasant in revolution. In particular he has explored the strange process by which peasant revolutions have given power to Marxists, whose theory of revolution is founded upon the urban proletariat.

I T is unlikely that anyone could have forecast the way in which the Revolution worked itself out, or indeed that anyone can as yet analyze soundly why and how things happened as they did. What is plain, and relevant to our subject, is that it was a double revolution — a peasant revolution and a political one; and while the peasant revolution at first took more or less its natural course, the other was given an accidental twist through the sudden injection of the Bolshevik element into the process of revolutionary gestation. Peasantism and Marxism were thus brought sharply face to face, not as before in a theoretical disputation but in a direct and purposeful issue of power. Trotsky has pointed out frankly in his brilliant *History of the Russian Revolution* all that divided the two categories in the stream of social evolution. In Russia, he wrote, the "chronic lag of ideas and relations behind new objective conditions," which creates "in a period of revolution that leaping movement of ideas and passions," was of a double kind. Russia's agrarian problem was still unsolved; the bourgeois revolution that had so profoundly affected France and England had had but small effect in Russia. "In order

to realize the Soviet State there was required a drawing together and mutual penetration of two factors belonging to completely different historic species: a peasant war — that is, a movement characteristic of the dawn of bourgeois development — and a proletarian insurrection, the movement signalizing its decline. That is the essence of 1917."

Herein lay the root of the many turns in Soviet agrarian policy, and in no small degree indeed of the Soviet system's whole dictatorial destiny. From the moment that Marxism, that is, analytical theory based on English conditions, gave place to Leninism, that is, revolutionary strategy based on the "objective situation" in eastern Europe, the issue of rent, which presupposes the existence of capitalist farming, was thrust into the background by the peasants' demand for land. Trotsky's historical distinction was in fact reflected strikingly in the attitude of the two revolutions on this issue. It was characteristic of Kerensky's "provisional" regime, with its bourgeois-liberal tendency, that it proposed to postpone agrarian reform till the convening of a national assembly. The government which took over after the October Revolution, however, at once

From David Mitrany, *Marx Against the Peasant: A Study in Social Dogmatism* (Chapel Hill, 1951), pp. 57–59. Reprinted by permission of The University of North Carolina Press and George Weidenfeld & Nicolson, Ltd.

handed over the land by decree to the peasants. Lenin had included the Left Social Revolutionaries in his government and had taken over their agrarian program, nationalization of all the land and its equal distribution among the peasants, though the Social Revolutionary group left it after only a few months.

There was indeed not much else that Lenin could do. The peasant revolution was well under way by the time the Bolsheviks staged their "proletarian" attack. From an admirable first-hand study of reports of local authorities Professor Robinson has shown that the rural revolution had spread quickly and effectively to all the provinces. The collapse of the old regime had been like a break in a dam, through which first a small trickle and then a rushing stream of spontaneous revolutionary action poured. The peasants began at once to take over forcibly large estates and forests, the number rising with every month — from 17 in March, 204 in April, 259 in May, 577 in June, to 1,122 in July. It was estimated that in the first two years the peasants in thirty-six departments had taken over 86 per cent of the large estates and 80 per cent of their farm equipment; this increased their holding from 80 to 96.8 per cent of all usable land.

But Yakovlev's description of the way in which the peasants dealt with the landlords also brought out clearly the non-political character of their revolt. The Bolsheviks, however, had reasons of their own not only for accepting the accomplished fact but for speeding the process. They had before then adopted the view that the simplest way to break the back of "feudal-bourgeois regimes" in the eastern countries was to let the peasants take over the land. At the particular moment, and in opposition to the Kerensky regime and its supporters, it was also a matter of policy with them to stop the "imperialist" war so as to let the revolutions which they implicitly expected in Germany and elsewhere get under way; and this fitted in with their urgent local need to prevent the army under its Tsarist officers from being turned against them. Though passive, the Russian armies were still holding the front, but they quickly disintegrated when the peasant soldiers heard that the land was theirs for the taking. One might perhaps sum it all up in this way, that 1917 was a diffused peasant revolution which the Bolsheviks took in hand and organized. They would indeed not have got very far had they not literally released and spurred the pent-up restlessness of the peasant masses. Evidence for this view is to be found in the political war of maneuver which for many years after they had to wage, and in the drastic means they finally had to use before they could bring to a head their own Bolshevik revolution.

The Peasant Became "Autocrat of Russia"

LAUNCELOT A. OWEN

Launcelot A. Owen, now a Senior Lecturer in History and Social Sciences at the Sydney Teachers' College, New South Wales, Australia, carried out his doctoral work at the London University School of Slavonic and East European Studies, where he worked with the late Sir Bernard Pares. His principal published work, *The Russian Peasant Movement, 1906–1917*, is a major contribution to knowledge about the peasant in revolution. His article here is a carefully documented study of the changing tenor of life in Russia's rural communities during 1917.

BY 3 April a new note of anxiety appeared in official documents. It was little more than a month since Nicholas II's abdication. The planting of seed for the harvest was imminent. Army and people depended upon that as on no other single economic factor. The Provisional Government issued an "appeal to citizens." That appeal received the support of the Soviet of Workers' and Soldiers' Deputies — which was symptomatic of the dyarchy which ruled in Petrograd until October. From the contents of the Minister's Circular one might assume that interference with estates in the vicinity of villages had already occurred, even if information upon that subject were not obtainable elsewhere.

The "tenour of village life" was deemed worthy of inquiry by the Central Government on 11 April. The suggested systemisation of reports itself conclusively reveals by internal evidence the various types of disorder that menaced authority over the length and breadth of the decaying Empire. An "agrarian movement" was now definitely recognised. Its phases were now catalogued — infringement of land laws; unauthorised acts affecting owners, landowners and land leaseholders; unauthorised ploughing of land; incendiarism; illicit timber-cutting; removal of farm implements; "cattle-lifting";

destruction of boundary marks; and, finally, trespassing.

To such qualitative analysis of the Russian agrarian situation, a quantitative survey is a useful supplement. Statistics which illuminate the period are to be extracted from *Information on the number and nature of violations of the law based on the sources of the Chief Administration of affairs of the Militia for March-September, 1917.* In March one finds only seventeen cases of infringement of land laws, whether implying attempted seizure of estates, interference with timber rights or the removal of labour from estates. Other general acts of criminal intent — involving burglary, robbery, deaths during disturbances, unauthorised arrests and searches, not to mention liberation of convicted prisoners — amounted to fifty-six cases. (The second figure is inclusive of urban disturbances.)

The month of April showed a considerable loosening of social discipline. Landed property rights were infringed in 204 cases. Yet cases of violence leading to fatal results or implying robbery or incitement of the populace to riot, amounted to 32 cases only. The figures for March and April cannot be directly compared, since some instances of violence were placed under the heading of landed-property infringements. Despite this

From L. A. Owen, "The Russian Agrarian Revolution of 1917," *The Slavonic and East European Review*, Vol. XII, No. 34 (July, 1933), pp. 156–66. By permission of Launcelot A. Owen and *The Slavonic and East European Review*.

minor reservation, the totals for March and April (73 and 236 cases, respectively) need little comment. A great change had evidently occurred in the countryside.

Numerous telegrams from private individuals told later of arrests and of the unauthorised activities of village communities. Cantonal committees, even before 13 April, were depriving landowners, both large and small, of "the possibility of executing their duty to the State." Undefined control over rural affairs was already exercised by the village communities themselves. A "land question" now appeared. An "unauthorised settlement" of this problem "in the interests of the population itself concerned in the matter" — a "fortuitous arrangement" governed solely by a "narrowly local point of view" — was a prospect upon which the administration of Prince Lvov could not but frown. The liberty of the individual, it appeared, no longer rested upon the sanctions of the old legal system. The consolidation of the new régime was menaced by unauthorised decrees — presumably of cantonal and village communities. It is abundantly clear that Provincial Commissaries had an unenviable task, suspended as they were in mid-air between a weakening authority above and the seething multitudes below. Dualism of government was not an unshared peculiarity of Petrograd.

As early as 6 May a fuel crisis had arisen — menacing both army and town. Local village committees were asserting a right as old as serfdom to the produce of forested areas in their neighbourhood. Yet it must not be imagined that peasant aggrandisement was the predominant factor in this crisis. Transport, of necessity, played an important part, as did the decreasing supplies of mineral fuel. It was the old Transport Regulations of 1916 that were now, in May 1917, invoked to cure a serious disease.

On 8 May the Provincial Commissaries were reminded that they must see "that the Central Government was always in touch with events." The first "All-Russian Peasant Congress" met in Petrograd in May. It must have been a matter of concern to Prince Lvov's Administration to know how far any potential radicalism among the delegates was likely to be supported in the villages. Lenin, too, was present, trying his ground and seeing what assistance his party might derive from the "radical bourgeois peasant who had not yet territorialised himself." The Bolshevik leader's reception at the Congress must have caused relief in the first post-revolutionary Cabinet. When Lenin advocated direct seizure of power, the assembled delegates are reported to have laughed. Strange how soon, in a revolutionary crisis, what seems ridiculous in spring will seem practicable in autumn!

Spirit depots[1] were causing disquiet before 9 May — riotous behaviour inevitably becoming even more dangerous in their vicinity. Yet the First Provisional Government was not inclined to allow the preventive destruction of such commercially valuable stores.

What directly affected the Army was the shortage, during March and April, of fodder. Brusilov, Commander-in-Chief of the Southwest Front, had already complained of its insufficiency.

If the picture presented in the Official Circular of 12 May is not exaggerated — and evidence from other sources does not lead one to suppose it can be — social dissolution was already not a potential but an actual phenomenon. Illegal arrests and searches, expulsion of estate staffs, destruction of estates, robberies and violence were the order of the day. "Respected officials" were no longer treated with respect. Various organisations were assuming governmental powers. Levies were being imposed by local authorities. Mobs were being incited to attack government representatives. Cleavages were appearing based on class, racial or religious distinctions.

Still more definite proof of Russia's dangerous position was the announcement that "wholesale desertions were rendering the Army impotent as a fighting force." That Army, one must not forget, was a peasant

[1] Government alcohol storage centers. [Editor's note]

Army. Desertions on such a scale were bound to increase the more militant elements of the villages that were soon to demand "Peace and Land."

Could Guchkov's successor, Kerensky, keep the Army on a military footing? Could Shingarev's successor, Chernov, assuage rural passions and hold in leash the peasant mastiff?

It is not often understood what a revolution was implied in the resignation of Prince Lvov (7 July). To have a Socialist Prime Minister gave Russia a unique position in the political world of Europe. To have a "narodnik" Minister of Agriculture was also an innovation, at which the worshippers of the popular communal land tenure in the sixties and seventies of the 19th century would have marvelled no less than their opponents. The more conservative elements of the First Provisional Government were willing to step aside if only the avowed representatives of (peasant) socialism could control the village — now almost uncontrollable. Could Russia be kept on a war-footing regardless of the disasters of the previous years? Or would 1917 prove to be the epilogue to the drama whose prologue had been 1905? Still more sand had to run through the glass before one could tell.

The head of the First Provisional Government publicly explained on 9 July the position which led to his resignation. His words are of import as indicating the failure of that Government's attempt to base itself upon personalities emanating from the last and fourth Duma of Nicholas II. It is certain that, in Prince Lvov's Administration, Milyukov and Guchkov had played, or had intended to play, more prominent parts. Yet it was the increasing impotence of the Government in agrarian affairs that drove Prince Lvov from office and, indirectly at least, gave the "trudovik"[2] Social Revolutionary, Kerensky, the reversion of the leadership.

"Although I believe" (wrote the retiring Prime Minister in the *Novoe Vremya* of

[2] trudovik: laborite. [Editor's note]

9 July) "that land ought to be handed over to the peasants, I cannot agree either with the content or the spirit of the land laws submitted by the Minister of Agriculture (i.e. Chernov) to the Provisional Government for ratification. The Provisional Government has declared that the occupation of the land should be organised in the interests of the working classes and of national welfare, but the Minister seems to me to depart from this principle and introduce laws which undermine the people's conception of justice. Far from combating aggressive tendencies or bringing order into agrarian relations, he appears to justify the disastrous seizures of property that are taking place throughout Russia and aims at confronting the Constituent Assembly with a *fait accompli*. To my mind, the laws proposed by him are part of a party programme and not measures necessary for the good of the country. I consider the Minister of Agriculture's land programme disastrous for the country, for it will ruin and undermine it both morally and materially, and I very much fear that it will create throughout Russia the state of things against which the Provisional Government has been, during the last few days, energetically struggling in Petrograd."

One is left in no doubt from the above letter that it was firstly the agrarian agitation and secondly the Social Revolutionary Party's increasing influence that caused Prince Lvov's withdrawal from office. Until July the advocates of a modernised "cherny peredel" (general redivision of all lands) stood behind the self-determination of the various cantonal and village assemblies of Russia. The views of Chernov, one of the principal theoreticians of the Party and the object of the retiring Prime Minister's attack, naturally form a subject of interest in the study of the period. At a lecture delivered on 30 April, 1917, in the Shanyavsky University, Moscow ("Agrarny vopros i sovremenny moment," reproduced in *Zemlya i Volya*, No. 44, Moscow), Chernov had re-emphasised a fact that everyone knew — that the Russian Army was a "peasant" — a "village army." Upon the village fell the burdens of the bloodshed. It was this "peasant army" that was especially interested in the land question. Rumours of land redistributions had even in the first two months after the revolution caused disquiet and desertions — desertions that threatened to impair the fighting-machine, already lacking in "morale" after the defeats of 1915 and the collapse of Roumania in the previous autumn. The emphasis of Chernov's remarks lay in his assertion that the agrarian question had a vital significance for the Army. The land question (he asserted) naturally stood in the centre of all the organised tasks of the moment. He considered that the prospective strength of labour democracy in the future Constituent Assembly would lead to another page in Russia's chronicle which should reproduce "the glorious history of the First and Second Dumas." He advised the slogan, "Land through the Constituent Assembly," while envisaging an elastic form of the oft-discussed "general redivision" based upon the labour capacity or actual size of the peasant family. His concluding declaration that "the peasantry itself was the real autocrat of Russia" ("Sam narod eto istinny Samoderzhets Rossii") was a statement the truth of which was never more evident than in the succeeding October, when he himself was hurled from power by those who utilised the forces that had placed his party in office.

If this article were not meant simply to summarise the main features of the peasant risings of 1917, it would be instructive to pursue the implications of the opposition of Lvov to Chernov — an opposition which showed that the forces of agrarian discontent were no longer latent. In fact, a new 1905 had dawned, this time considerably magnified.

The quantitative significance of the peasant aggrandisement in May and June certainly gave the First Provisional Government little cause for optimism. Compared with the 204 cases in April, May provided 259 cases of law-breaking in landed property relationships. In contrast with the 32 cases recorded in April of violence or destruction involving person or property, there were 152 cases in May. The month of June certainly showed no decrease in the first type of offence, of which there were 577 instances. Of the second type, however, a decrease is recorded, there being 112 instances.

It was in July, however, the month when the more conservative elements were in retreat, leaving the agrarian socialists and moderate Social Democrats masters of the field, that the alarming total of 1,122 cases was registered as the number of infringements of landed property rights in the Russian dominions. Of this amount, 1,100 instances occurred in European Russia alone. Seizure of property or assault upon the person represented 387 cases, of which the majority (342) were again in Europe.

It may be pertinent to note here that the "organised" or "inspired" nature of the peasant movements had now reached its acme. The more moderate Social Revolutionaries, as champions of peasant rights, were necessarily no longer interested in stirring up the peasantry against a government whose leader, Kerensky, was their own man and in which their ideas were admittedly predominant. Yet later months, from August to October, were to make it questionable whether the nominally triumphant party had in fact led the agrarian offensive. One might be forgiven for supposing that they had simply walked in front of spontaneously advancing hosts. It was certainly no easy task to control the peasant rear when the efforts of the new head of the Provisional Government had so signally failed to galvanise the front into a patriotic offensive.

On 18 July, H. G. Tsereteli,[3] not long returned from his Siberian exile to which he had been despatched with other socialist members of the Second Duma ten years before, issued an appeal for order in rural areas. The conditions reported to him from

[3] Then Minister of the Interior. [Editor's note]

the countryside menaced "the army, the country and the existence of the State itself." Proceeding, he declared that "Revolutionary Russia must be secured from hostile action without and cold and hunger within." He deprecated illegal redivisions of land which, he stated, threatened the food and fuel supplies. But despite the ability of Kerensky and Tsereteli to control the capital, the thousands of village communities were a different proposition.

July witnessed the culmination of peasant self-determination as far as it was encouraged by parties, such as that of the Social Revolutionaries, or by persons speaking in that party's name. For every hundred cases of peasant infringement of the old legal arrangements, March had reported only six to be inspired. In April, 33 cases were supposed to be of organised character. May announced 67 instances of that type; June, 86; July, 120.

The Social Revolutionary Party, together with its Social Democratic allies (or the representatives of these parties in power), considered the prosecution of the war of greater moment than the drastic rearrangement of the social and economic relations of the village. The Government now relied upon "the fulness of its revolutionary authority to preserve the whole land fund unimpaired until the convocation of the All-Russian Constituent Assembly which will transfer the land into the hands of those working it." If one recalls the pre-revolutionary decade and the stormy debates of the First Duma, one understands fully the social implications of the above announcement. To quell peasant disturbances and to persuade the war-weary army to resume the conflict at the Front, the Government categorically adopted the programme of the "Trudoviki" (Labour Group) of Russia's first modern parliament. Certainly the prospective redistribution rested with the so far unconvened legislature. The cantonal and village assemblies were offered a promissory note to be honoured later. The value received was to be renewed

peasant support of the war-aims of the Second Provisional Government.

Simultaneously the Government challenged the authority of the multiplicity of "executive committees" that had sprung mushroom-like from the soil of Russia at Nicholas II's abdication. Of these spontaneously acting bodies the Soviet in Petrograd was but one. Cantonal committees were now ubiquitous. Provincial and District Commissaries were becoming either figureheads or puppets in their hands. The Food and Land Committees, responsible to their central bodies in the capital, were, indeed, recognised by the Government. It was in fact A. I. Shingarev, a Constitutional Democrat (Liberal), who had promulgated the decree that instituted them. Chernov, his successor, followed in his footsteps. These Food and Land Committees found little support locally, save where their personnel either coincided with, or was controlled by, the cantonal or village executive committees. The inability of the Central Government to guide these local committees led to the ultimate elimination of Kerensky and Chernov in October.

The ensuing months witnessed a series of attempts to restore the authority of Petrograd over Russia by the application of military force. General Kornilov now (on 31 July) made generally applicable to the whole war zone a "Compulsory Decree" (No. 737) which had originally been declared, on 8 July, to cover only the Southwestern Front. Railway transport, the Commander-in-Chief asserted, was in ruins. Food for the troops and forage for the animals was still deficient. "The agrarian question can in no wise be decided in unauthorised fashion with the use of violence."

Whether the cause lay in the increased firmness of the Central Government's handling of affairs, as witnessed by the above decree, or whether the requirements of harvesting turned village minds to their usual economic labours, there did occur a decrease in the number of reported cases of rural illegalities. Whereas July had shown

1,122 breaches of land laws, August reported only 691. On the contrary, acts of seizure accompanied by violence increased from 387 in July to 440 in August.

The question of the gathering of the harvest now (by 2 September) caused anxiety in Petrograd. The Minister of Agriculture, Chernov, required Provincial and District Commissaries to prevent any interference in that operation by cantonal committees. On 26 August, General Kornilov made his premature attempt to seize Petrograd and stay the progress of revolutionary events. His action and the subsequent loss of prestige which Kerensky experienced actually helped to "deepen" the Revolution and make certain future events almost inevitable. The army continued to disintegrate. The garrisons in the rear showed less and less inclination to act against their village compatriots.

On 8 September, Kerensky, in his capacity of Prime Minister and Commander-in-Chief, reiterated what the now deposed Kornilov had earlier decreed. There was clearly increasing anarchy in every sphere of rural life. A food and fuel crisis threatened both front and rear. Local Commissaries were definitely instructed to apply for military assistance if necessary.

If account is taken of the numerical value of the breaches of land laws in September, it is found that the previously-mentioned decline in August continued in the succeeding month. The August total of 691 cases sank to 629 in September. Harvesting, as before, probably affected the figures. Yet the number of cases of seizure accompanied by violence — certainly a truer reflex of the Government's weakness and of the loosening of social bonds — rose from 440 in August to 958 in the next month.

October presented a catastrophic appearance. A state of civil war virtually existed. The Ministry of the Interior, at this date under N. D. Avksentyev, recognised that "the internal position of the country is continually growing weaker" (7 October). Commissaries were asked to endeavour "to unite the well-disposed elements of the population in the fight against increasing anarchy." The "active support of the population" was essential. Certainly that was the one factor that the Government had failed to secure. "The foreign enemy (it was proclaimed) was penetrating further and further into the heart of the country." The Government was convinced that "all must experience immediate alarm over the disorders which were happening everywhere in the wildest forms." The Russian people "did not show any signs of a protective instinct (spasitelnovo podema) which love of country, dread for its fate and a sense of self-preservation should inspire." Inertia among the villagers menaced the authority of the Provisional Government. Every social organisation should be asked to cooperate with the Provincial Commissaries in restoring order. The new cantonal *zemstva* were one of the expedients on which Petrograd counted to retain peasant loyalty. But that new institution — despite its basis of universal suffrage — could not withstand the village executive committees.

As a last despairing hope it was announced that "selected and trustworthy military men, released from service or given leave to join," were to supplement the notoriously feeble militia. The peasantry sank into a political coma from which the prospective loss of its gains during the year under review alone could awaken it almost twelve months later.

Even parish churches were exposed to attack. Monastic and church land had not escaped expropriation during the period of the supremacy of local executive committees. So alarming had the situation become that the Militia Department now (on 7 October) instructed the Commissaries that the provisions of the "General Act Governing the Peasant Estate," as set forth in the Collection of Laws (Svod Zakonov), should be utilised "to compel village communities to maintain guards over local churches and monasteries." Had the old and oft-quoted peasant esteem for the religion of his fathers failed to survive in the general chaos? One can draw no other conclusion.

Upon the question of the danger to the public peace owing to the riotous destruction of spirit stores it appears that even on the eve of the fatal 25 October the Government hesitated to sanction their official demolition in view of the consequent financial loss to the Treasury.

Even more disquieting was the food situation. The "consuming" provinces (not to mention Petrograd and Moscow) feared starvation. The provinces of the south and east that produced a grain surplus were unable to secure adequate manufactured articles to warrant a continuance of internal trade. The *quid pro quo* was absent. This breakdown of economic relations menaced what little chance there was of maintaining the active army at the Front. Military assist-ance was offered to the local Commissaries, who were to employ troops at double the usual rates. The result resembled that which met Canute when he rebuked the waves. Even reinforcements in the form of reserve regiments failed to stem the tide of rural rebellion.

The month of October provided 42.1 per cent of the total number of cases of destructive activity registered since Nicholas II's fall from power. The number of estates affected by the agrarian movement increased in September by 30.2 per cent over August, and, in October, by 43.2 per cent over September. The period of pseudo-legality, of ostensibly legal sequestration of private estates, gave place in the last two months of Kerensky's administration to one of real peasant war.

National Minorities Sought Autonomy
and Independence

RICHARD PIPES

Born in Poland in 1923, Richard Pipes completed his formal studies
at Harvard University, where he is now an Associate Professor in History.
The political aspects of the nationality movements of the Soviet Union
have been his special interest for nearly a decade, and the work from
which the selection here is taken is a brilliant contribution to our knowledge of developments in this field during and immediately after the
revolution. In recent years Professor Pipes has published several new
articles on the nationalities problem and has written on Russian conservative thought.

THE Russian Empire, as it appeared in
1917, was the product of nearly four
centuries of continuous expansion. Unlike
other European nations, Russia was situated
on the edge of the vast Asiatic mainland
and knew relatively few geographic deter-
rents to aggrandizement. This geographi-
cally favorable situation was made even
more advantageous by the political weakness of Russia's neighbors, who were especially ineffective on the eastern and southern
frontiers. Here vast and potentially rich
territories were either under the dominion
of internally unstable and technologically
backward Moslem principalities, or else
sparsely populated by nomadic and semi-
nomadic groups without any permanent
political institutions whatsoever — forces incapable of long range resistance to the
pressures of a large and dynamic state.
Hence Russia, somewhat like the United
States, found outlets for expansive tendencies along its own borders instead of
overseas. The process of external growth
had been rapid, beginning with the inception of the modern Russian state and developing in close connection with it. It has
been estimated that the growth of the
Russian Empire between the end of the
fifteenth and the end of the nineteenth
century proceeded at the rate of 130 square
kilometers or fifty square miles a day.

Almost from its very inception the Moscow state had acquired dominion over non-
Russian peoples. Ivan the Terrible conquered Kazan and Astrakhan and brought
the state a large number of Turks (Volga
Tatars, Bashkirs) and Finns (Chuvashes,
Mordvinians) from the region of the Volga
River and its tributaries. In the seventeenth
century, the tsars added Siberia, populated
by Turkic, Mongol, and Finnish tribes. The
left-bank regions of the Dnieper River, with
their Cossack population — the forerunners
of modern Ukrainians — came under a
Russian protectorate in 1654. During the
eighteenth century, moving west, Peter the
Great conquered from Sweden the eastern
shores of the Baltic Sea (today's Estonia
and Latvia), while Catherine the Great, as
a result of agreements with Austria and
Prussia, seized the eastern provinces of the
Polish-Lithuanian Commonwealth. Catherine's successful wars with Turkey brought
Russia possession of the northern shores of
the Black Sea, including the Crimean pen-

Reprinted by permission of the publishers from Richard Pipes, *The Formation of the Soviet Union:
Communism and Nationalism, 1917–1923* (Cambridge, Mass.: Harvard Univerity Press), pp. 1–8,
50–53. Copyright 1954 by The President and Fellows of Harvard College.

63

insula. The Transcaucasian Kingdom of Eastern Georgia was incorporated in 1801, Finland in 1809, and the central regions of Poland in 1815. The remainder of Transcaucasia and the Northern Caucasus were acquired in the first half of the century, and Alexander II added most of Turkestan.

The first systematic census, undertaken in 1897, revealed that the majority (55.7 per cent) of the population of the Empire, exclusive of the Grand Duchy of Finland, consisted of non-Russians. The total population of the Empire was 122,666,500. The principal groups were divided, by native language, as follows (the figures are in per cent):

Slavs	
Great Russians	44.32
Ukrainians	17.81
Poles	6.31
Belorussians	4.68
Turkic peoples	10.82
Jews	4.03
Finnish peoples	2.78
Lithuanians and Latvians	2.46
Germans	1.42
Caucasian Mountain peoples (gortsy)	1.34
Georgians	1.07
Armenians	0.93
Iranian peoples	0.62
Mongolians	0.38
Others	1.03

One of the anomalies of pre-1917 Russia was the fact that although, to quote one observer, "the Russian Empire, Great Russian in its origin, ceased being such in its ethnic composition," the state, with some exceptions, continued to be treated constitutionally and administratively as a nationally homogeneous unit. The principle of autocracy, preserved in all its essentials until the Revolution of 1905, did not permit — at least in theory — the recognition of separate historic or national territories within the state in which the monarch's authority would be less absolute or rest on a legally different basis from that which he exercised at home. In practice, however, this principle was not always consistently applied. At various times in history Russian tsars did

grant considerable autonomy to newly conquered territories, partly in recognition of their special status, partly in anticipation of political reforms in Russia, and in some cases they even entered into contractual relations with subject peoples, thus limiting their own power.

Poland from 1815 to 1831 and Finland from 1809 to 1899 were in theory as well as in practice constitutional monarchies. Other regions, such as the Ukraine from 1654 to 1764, Livonia and Estonia from 1710 to 1783 and from 1795 to the 1880's, enjoyed extensive self-rule. But those exceptions were incompatible with the maintenance of the principle of autocracy in Russia itself. Sooner or later, for one reason or another, the privileges granted to conquered peoples were retracted, contracts were unilaterally abrogated, and the subjects, together with their territories, were incorporated into the regular administration of the Empire.

At the close of the nineteenth century, Finland alone still retained a broad measure of self-rule. Indeed, in some respects, it possessed greater democratic rights than Russia proper; Finland under the tsars presented the paradox of a subject nation possessing more political freedom than the people who ruled over it. It was a separate principality, which the Russian monarch governed in his capacity as Grand Duke (Velikii kniaz'). The tsar was the chief executive; he controlled the Grand Duchy's foreign affairs; he decided on questions of war and peace; he approved laws and the appointments of judges. The tsar also named the resident Governor General of the Grand Duchy, who headed the Finnish and Russian armies and the police on its territory, and who was responsible for the appointments of local governors. A State Secretary served as the intermediary between the Russian monarch and the Finnish organs of self-rule. The Finns had complete control over the legislative institutions of the state. They possessed a bicameral legislative body, composed of a Senate and a Seim (Diet). The Senate considered legislative projects and performed the function of the supreme court of the state. The Seim was the highest legislative organ in the country. Called every five years on the basis of nation-wide elections, it initiated and voted on legislation pertaining to its domain. No law could become effective without its approval. Finnish citizens in addition enjoyed other privileges. Every Finnish subject, while in Russia proper, could claim all the rights of Russian citizens, although Russian citizens in Finland were considered foreigners. In every respect, therefore, Finland had a uniquely privileged position in the Russian Empire, which resembled more closely the dominion relationship in existence in the British Empire than the customary colonial relationship prevalent in other parts of Russia. The Finns had originally acquired these privileges from the Swedes, who had ruled their country before the Russian conquest. The tsars preserved them because Finland was acquired by Alexander I, a monarch of relatively liberal views, who, for a time, had thought of introducing a constitutional regime into Russia proper.

Prior to 1917, the Russian Empire also possessed two protectorates, the Central Asian principalities of Bukhara and Khiva. In 1868 and 1873 respectively, these states recognized the sovereignty of the Russian tsar and ceded to him the right to represent them in relations with other powers. They also granted Russians exclusive commercial privileges and were compelled to abolish slavery in their domains. Otherwise, they enjoyed self-rule.

The remaining borderlands of the Empire were administered, in the last decades of the *ancien régime,* in a manner which did not differ essentially — though it differed in some particulars — from that in effect in the territories of Russia proper. Whatever special powers the Imperial Government deemed necessary to grant to the authorities administering these territories were derived not so much from a recognition of the multinational character of the state or from a desire to adapt political institutions to the needs of the inhabitants, as from the im-

practicability of extending the administrative system of the Great Russian provinces in its entirety to the borderland.

Whereas, for example, Russia was divided into provinces (*gubernie*), administered by governors, most of the borderland areas were grouped into General Gubernie, which included anywhere from a few to a dozen regular provinces, and were headed by governors general, usually high army officers. The distance of the borderlands from the center, the sparsity of population in some and the existence of strong nationalist traditions in others, required that the persons administering such areas be granted greater powers than was necessary in the central provinces of the Empire. The governor general was a viceroy, with extraordinary powers to maintain order and to suppress revolutionary activity. He had a right to employ any means necessary to the performance of his duty, including arrests or expulsions without recourse to courts. In some regions, the governor general also received additional powers, required by local conditions. There were ten such governors general: in Warsaw (with jurisdiction over ten Polish provinces), in Kiev (with jurisdiction over the Ukraine, or Little Russia, including the provinces of Kiev, Volhynia, and Podolia), in Vilna (today's Lithuania and Belorussia, with the provinces of Vilna, Grodno, and Kovno), two in Central Asia (Turkestan and Steppe), and two in Siberia (the so-called Irkutskoe, and Priamurskoe). The Governor General of Finland, although bearing the title, had in effect very little authority, and could not be classed in the same category as the other governors general. The official heading the administration of the Caucasus, on the other hand, while formally called a viceroy, was for all practical purposes a full-fledged governor general. The city of Moscow, because of its importance and central location, also formed a general guberniya.

Under the governor general were the provincial governors who had to communicate with the central political institutions of the Empire through him, but who, as a rule, were called "military governors" (*voennye gubernatory*), and had both civil and military jurisdiction. The military governors of Turkestan were directly appointed by the Russian Ministry of War.

The gubernie, or provinces, were — as elsewhere in Russia — further subdivided into districts (*okruga,* or less commonly *uezdy*), but in the eastern borderlands such circumscriptions generally embraced much larger territories and had a simpler structure. On the lowest administrative level there existed considerable variety. In some regions, the population was divided into villages or *auly;* in others, where the inhabitants were nomadic, they were organized into tribes; in yet others, they were administered together with the local Russian population.

Russian law also made special provisions for certain groups of non-Russian subjects. Russia, prior to 1917, retained the system of legally recognized classes and class privileges, long since defunct in Western Europe. Within this system there was a social category of so-called *inorodtsy,* a term which has no exact equivalent in English and can best be rendered by the French *peuples allogènes.* The inorodtsy comprised the Jews and most of the nomadic peoples of the Empire, who were subject to special laws rather than to the general laws promulgated in the territories which they inhabited. For the nomadic inorodtsy, this meant in effect that they possessed the right to self-rule, with their native courts and tribal organization. Their relations with the Russian authorities were limited to the payment of a fixed tribute or tax, usually to an agent of the Ministry of Interior or of State Properties. By settling on land and abandoning nomadic habits, an inorodets changed from his status to that of a regular Russian citizen, with all the duties and privileges of the class which he had joined; as long as he retained his inorodets status, he gave nothing to the government and received nothing in return. Russian treatment of the nomads was, on the whole, characterized by tolerance and respect for native traditions. Much of the credit for

this must be given to the great liberal statesman, M. M. Speranskii, who, at the beginning of the nineteenth century, had laid down the basic principles for their administration.

For the other subgroup of inorodtsy, the Jews, membership in this class entailed stringent restrictions (most of them stemming from eighteenth-century legislation). These forbade them to move out of a strictly defined area in the southwestern and northwestern parts of the Empire, the so-called Pale of Settlement, to purchase landed property, or to settle outside the towns. Such disabilities brought severe social and economic suffering, for the Jews were crowded into towns where they had no adequate basis for livelihood and had to rely heavily on primitive handicraftsmanship and petty trade to survive. By creating abnormal economic conditions in the Jewish communities and preventing them from taking their place in the life of society, the restrictive legislation contributed to the large number of Jews found in radical movements at the beginning of the twentieth century. The Jew could alter his status only by adopting Christianity.

At no point in its history did tsarist Russia formulate a consistent policy toward the minorities. In the early period of the Empire, approximately from the middle of the sixteenth until the middle of the eighteenth century, the attitude of the government toward its non-Russian subjects was influenced strongly by religion. Where discrimination existed, the principal reason was the desire of the regime to convert Moslems, Jews, and other non-Christians to the Orthodox faith. Toward the end of the eighteenth century, with the secularization of the Russian monarchy, this religious element lost its force, and political considerations loomed ever larger. Thereafter, the treatment of the minorities, as of the Great Russians themselves, was largely determined by the desire on the part of the monarchs to maintain and enforce the principle of autocracy; minority groups which challenged this effort in the name of national rights were treated as harshly as were Russian groups which challenged it in the name of democracy or freedom in general.

The period from the accession of Alexander III (1881) to the outbreak of the 1905 Revolution was that in which persecution of the minorities culminated. The Russian government perhaps for the first time in its entire history adopted a systematic policy of Russification and minority repression, largely in an endeavor to utilize Great Russian national sentiments as a weapon against growing social unrest in the country. During this period, Finnish privileges were violated through a suspension of the legislative powers of the Seim (1899), the introduction of the compulsory study of Russian in Finnish secondary schools, the subordination of the Finnish Ministry of Post and Telegraphs to the corresponding Russian institution, and other restrictive measures. Polish cultural activity was severely limited; the Jewish population was subjected to pogroms inspired or tolerated by the government, and to further economic restrictions (for instance, the revocation of the right to distill alcohol); the Ukrainian cultural movement was virtually brought to a standstill as a result of the prohibitions imposed on printing in the Ukrainian language (initiated in the 1870's); the properties of the Armenian church were confiscated by the Viceroy of the Caucasus (1903). It was, however, not accidental that this era of Russification coincided with the period of greatest governmental reaction, during which the Great Russian population itself lost many of the rights which it had acquired in the Great Reforms of Alexander II (1856–1881).

The outbreak of the Revolution of 1905 and the subsequent establishment of a constitutional monarchy brought to a halt the period of national persecution but it did not repair all the damage done in the previous quarter-century. The Dumas, especially the First, in which the minorities were well represented, gave only slight attention to the national question, though they provided an open rostrum of discussions on that topic. In 1907, the government regained supremacy over the liberal elements; it changed the electoral laws in favor of the Russian upper classes, among whom supporters of the autocracy were strong, depriving the remainder of the population of a proportionate voice in the legislative institutions of the state. The borderlands, where liberal and socialist parties enjoyed a particularly strong following, were hardest hit by the change, and some (Turkestan, for instance) lost entirely the right to representation.

NATIONAL MOVEMENTS IN RUSSIA

The paradox — and tragedy — of Russian history in the last century of the *ancien régime* was the fact that while the government clung to the anachronistic notion of absolutism, the country itself was undergoing an extremely rapid economic, social, and intellectual evolution, which required new, more flexible forms of administration. The nineteenth century was a period when capitalism and the industrial revolution penetrated Russia, stimulating the development of some social classes which had previously been weak (a middle class, an industrial proletariat, and a prosperous, land-owning peasantry), and undermining others (e.g., the landed aristocracy). Western ideas, such as liberalism, socialism, nationalism, utilitarianism, now found a wide audience in Russia. The Russian monarchy, which until the nineteenth century had been the principal exponent of Western ideas in Russia, now lagged behind. The second half of the reign of Alexander I (1815–1825) marked the beginning of that rift between the monarchy and the articulate elements in Russian society which, widening continuously, led to conspiratorial movements, terrorist activity, and revolution, and finally, in 1917, to the demise of monarchy itself.

The national movement among the minorities of the Russian state, which also began in the nineteenth century, represented one of the many forms which this intellectual and social ferment assumed.

Because the traditions and socio-economic interests of the various groups of subjects, including the minorities, were highly diversified, their cultural and political development tended to take on a local, and in some cases, a national coloring. Romantic philosophy, which first affected Russia in the 1820's, stimulated among the minority intellectuals an interest in their own languages and past traditions, and led directly to the evolution of cultural nationalism, the first manifestation of the national movement in the Russian borderlands.

Next, in the 1860's and 1870's, the spread of Russian Populism, with its emphasis on the customs and institutions of the peasantry, provided the minority intellectuals with a social ideology and induced them to establish contact with the broad masses of their own, predominantly rural, population. Finally, the development of modern political parties in Russia, which took place about 1900, led to the formation of national parties among the minorities, which in almost all instances adopted either liberal or socialist programs and affiliated themselves closely with their Russian counterparts. Until the breakdown of the tsarist regime, such Russian and minority parties fought side by side for parliamentary rights, local self-rule, and social and economic reforms; but while the Russian parties stressed the general needs of the whole country, the minority parties concentrated on local, regional requirements. The fact that the minorities in Russia developed a national consciousness before their fellow-nationals across the border (the Ukrainians in Austrian Galicia, Armenians in the Ottoman Empire, Azerbaijanis in Persia, and so on), was a result of the more rapid intellectual and economic growth of the Russian Empire.

The refusal of the tsarist regime to recognize the strivings of the minorities was part of the larger phenomenon of its failure to respond to the growing clamor on the part of all its citizens for fundamental reforms, and had equally dire results.

*   *   *

The outbreak of the Russian Revolution had, as its initial consequence, the abolition of the tsarist regime and, as its ultimate result, the complete breakdown of all forms of organized life throughout Russia. One of the aspects of this breakdown was the disintegration of the Empire and the worsening of relations between its various ethnic groups. In less than a year after the Tsar had abdicated, the national question had become an outstanding issue in Russian politics.

Immediately after resuming power, the Provisional Government issued decrees which abolished all restrictive legislation imposed on the minorities by the tsarist regime, and established full equality of all citizens regardless of religion, race, or national origin. The government also introduced the beginnings of national self-rule by placing the administration of the borderlands in the hands of prominent local figures. Transcaucasia and Turkestan were put under the jurisdiction of special committees, composed largely of Duma deputies of native nationalities, to replace the governors general of the tsarist administration. The southwestern provinces were put in charge of Ukrainians, though the government refused to recognize the existence of the entire Ukraine as an administrative unit until forced to do so under Ukrainian pressure in the summer of 1917. Those were pioneering steps in the direction of adapting the governmental machinery to the multinational character of the Empire and giving the minorities a voice in the administration of their territories, but unfortunately the local committees to which the Provisional Government had relegated authority possessed very little real power, and after the summer of 1917 functioned only nominally.

The Provisional Government considered itself a temporary trustee of state sovereignty, and viewed its main task as that of preserving unity and order until the people should have an opportunity to express its own will in the Constituent Assembly. Throughout its existence the government resisted as well as it could all pressures to enact legislation which might affect the constitution of the state. Any such measures it regarded as an infringement on popular sovereignty. This attitude, sound from the moral and constitutional points of view, proved fatal as political practice. The February Revolution had set into motion forces which would not wait. The procrastinating policies of the Provisional Government led to growing anarchy which Lenin and his followers, concentrating on the seizure of power and unhampered by any moral scruples or constitutional considerations, utilized to accomplish a successful *coup d'état*.

The growth of the national movements in Russia during 1917, and especially the unexpectedly rapid development of political aspirations on the part of the minorities, were caused to a large extent by the same factors which in Russia proper made possible the triumph of Bolshevism: popular restlessness, the demand for land and peace, and the inability of the democratic government to provide firm authority.

The growing impatience of the rural population with delays in the apportionment of land which caused the peasantry of the ethnically Great Russian provinces to turn against the government and to attack large estates, had different effects in the eastern borderlands. There the dissatisfaction of the native population was not so much directed against the landlord as against the Russian colonist; it was he who had deprived the native nomad of his grazing grounds and with the aid of Cossack or Russian garrisons had kept the native from the land which he considered his own by inheritance. When the February Revolution broke out, the native population of the Northern Caucasus, the Ural region and much of the steppe districts of Central Asia expected that the new democracy would at once remedy the injustices of the past by returning to them the properties of which they had been deprived. When this did not happen, they took matters into their own hands, and tried to seize land by force.

But in doing so they encountered the resistance of Russian and Cossack villages. Thus, in the second half of the year, while a class struggle was taking place in Russia proper, an equally savage national conflict developed in the vast eastern borderlands of the Empire: Chechen and Ingush against Russian and Cossack; Kazakh-Kirghiz against the Russian and Ukrainian colonist; Bashkir against the Russian and Tatar.

In the Ukraine, too, the agricultural question assumed a national form although for quite different reasons. The Ukrainian peasants, especially the rural middle class, found it advantageous, as will be seen, in view of the superiority of the soil in their provinces, to solve the land question independently of Russia proper.

War-weariness was another factor which tended to increase nationalist emotions. Non-Russian soldiers, like their Russian comrades, desired to terminate the fighting and to return home. Uncertain how to go about it, they organized their own military formations and military councils, hoping in this manner to be repatriated sooner, and to obtain by common action a better response to their demands. By the end of the year the formation of such national units had increased to the point where non-Russian troops, abandoning the front, frequently returned to their homes as a body. Once on their native soil, they augmented native political organizations and provided them with military power. The national movement in 1917 had perhaps its most rapid development in the army.

The Bolsheviks, inciting Russian peasants and soldiers against the government, were persuasive in contending that the government did not grant their demands because it had become a captive of the "bourgeoisie." The non-Russian, on the other hand, could be led to believe that the trouble lay not so much in the class-character of the Provisional Government, as in its ethnic composition. Nationalistic parties in some areas began to foster the idea that all Russian governments, autocratic as well as democratic, were inspired by the same hostility toward the minorities and should be equally mistrusted.

Immediately after the fall of the *ancien régime* the minorities, like the Russians, established local organs of internal self-rule. The original purpose of these institutions was to serve as centers of public discussion for the forthcoming Constituent Assembly and to attend to non-political affairs connected with the problems of local administration. Whether called Soviet, Rada (in the Ukraine and Belorussia), *Shura* (among the Turkic peoples), or their equivalents in other native languages, they were originally not intended to infringe upon the authority of the Provisional Government. In time, however, as the authority of the Provisional Government declined, these organs acquired a correspondingly greater voice in local affairs. At first they only assumed responsibility over supply and communication, the maintenance of public order, and, in some cases, the defense of their territories from external enemies — services which Petrograd could not provide. But at the end of 1917, when, as a result of the Bolshevik coup, a political vacuum was created in the country, they appropriated sovereignty itself. While the soviets, largely under the influence of the Bolsheviks and left SR's, proclaimed the overthrow of the Provisional Government and the establishment of rule of the Congress of Soviets, the minority organizations took over the responsibilities of government for their own peoples and the territories which they inhabited. These local organs of administration which arose in the borderlands during the October Revolution and succeeding months were based on the principle of national self-rule and functioned alone or in condominium with the soviets.

For a time it seemed possible that these national organs would cooperate with the new Russian government. In the initial period of Communist rule no one knew how the new regime would treat the minorities. But before long it became apparent that the Soviet government had no intention of respecting the principle of national self-determination and that in spreading its authority it was inclined to utilize social forces hostile to minority interests. In the Ukraine, it favored that part of the industrial proletariat which was, by ethnic origin and sympathy, oriented toward Russia and inimical to the striving of the local peasantry; in the Moslem areas, the colonizing elements and the urban population composed largely of Russian newcomers; in Transcaucasia and Belorussia, the deserting Russian troops. The triumph of Bolshevism was interpreted in many borderland areas as the victory of the city over the village, the worker over the peasant, the Russian colonist over the native.

It was under such circumstances that the national councils, bolstered by sentiments which had matured in the course of the year, proclaimed their self-rule, and in some instances, their complete independence.

Bolsheviks Led Workers toward Radical Revolution

ISAAC DEUTSCHER

Isaac Deutscher was born in Poland and educated at Cracow. He engaged in journalistic work in Poland from 1924 until 1939, and was a member of the Polish Communist Party until 1932, when he was expelled for anti-Stalinist opposition. He has continued his journalistic activities in London since 1939 and has written several excellent studies on Russian affairs. Among his best-known books in this field are: *Soviet Trade Unions; The Prophet Armed, Trotsky, 1879–1921;* and the justly famous *Stalin,* from which the following selection is taken. The latter is undoubtedly the most exhaustive and balanced study of Stalin yet written.

DURING May and June the revolutionary fever in Petersburg continually mounted. Municipal elections in the capital exposed the weakness of Miliukov's Constitutional Democrats (Cadets), the party that predominated in the Government. Half the vote went to the moderate Socialists, leaving the two extreme parties, Cadets and Bolsheviks, as influential minorities. The predominantly Cadet Government gave way to a coalition of Cadets, Mensheviks, and Social Revolutionaries. But the new Government as it tried to ride the storm showed few signs of real strength. The Bolsheviks were becoming the masters in the working-class suburbs of Petersburg. From the army came the ever louder clamour for peace, while Russia's western allies were pressing the Russian Supreme Command to start an all-out offensive against the Germans. The Bolsheviks met the new coalition with grim hostility; but in opposing it they displayed a tactical imagination and subtlety which could not fail to yield massive and quick rewards. They did not simply shout down the whole Government, for they knew that the working class was still favourably impressed by the fact that Socialist parties were now in office, for the first time in Russian history. But the working classes were also suspicious of the middle-class Cadets, the senior partners in the coalition. Lenin therefore pressed the moderate Socialists to break up the coalition and form a Government of their own, based on the Soviets. In the Red suburbs of the capital hosts of Bolshevik agitators raised two plain slogans: "Down with the Ten Capitalist Ministers!" and "All Power to the Soviets!" The first slogan stirred the widespread suspicion of the Cadets common to the Menshevik and Bolshevik rank and file. The demand that all power be transferred to the Soviets was equivalent to the demand that the moderate Socialists should take power alone, since they wielded a majority in the Soviets; and so that slogan, too, had its appeal to the ordinary Menshevik worker. Throughout May and June, legions of Menshevik workers were converted to Bolshevism. On 18 June half a million workers and soldiers marched in the streets of the capital in a procession which was nominally called by the Menshevik leaders of the Soviets. The vast mass of demonstrators carried placards and banners with almost exclusively Bolshevik slogans. The first All-Russian Congress of Soviets was just then in session; and the delegates from the provinces, among whom the Bolsheviks were still a minority of one-sixth, could not help being impressed by this demonstration of Bolshevik influence in the capital.

At the Congress of the Soviets there occurred a significant incident. When one of the Socialist ministers was apologetically explaining the need for a broadly based government and arguing that no party could cope single-handed with the disintegration and chaos engendered by the war, Lenin, from the floor, interrupted the speaker with a curt statement that his party was ready to assume the whole power. Lenin's words were received with loud, derisive laughter; but the mass processions in the streets of the capital imparted to them a deadly earnestness.

In fact, the Bolsheviks were not yet ready to take power. They continued to regard the Soviets as the legitimate source of revolutionary authority; and, as long as his party was in a minority in the Soviets, Lenin ruled out any attempt on its part at seizing power. But he had to work hard to keep on a leash the impatient, semi-anarchist groups of workers, soldiers, and sailors who fretted at his prudent tactics. He saw that his scheme of action was imperilled by the uneven rhythm and impetus of the revolution. While his policies were still too extreme for the provincial working class, a large section of the garrison and the proletariat in the capital was already beginning to suspect the Bolsheviks, too, of excessive moderation or of insufficient revolutionary pluck. In *Pravda* Stalin was compelled to warn the Red suburbs against the anarchist and semi-anarchist agitators who urged the workers to "come out" prematurely. In the next few months Bolshevism uneasily balanced between the hazards of delaying the revolution and the risks of premature action.

The hazards and risks were increased by the fact that the counter-revolution, too, was preparing for a show-down. Monarchist generals, leagues of patriotic officers, associations of ex-service men and the Cadet middle class, all took notice of the meaning of the June demonstration and made up their minds to throw back the mounting tide of Bolshevism by a violent *coup*. The moderate Socialist leaders were intimidated and vaguely played with the idea that such a show-down would rid them of their rivals on the left, against whom they themselves were more and more helpless. Lenin and his colleagues were determined not to allow themselves to be driven into premature insurrection. They were fairly confident that, basing themselves on the proletarian masses of the capital alone, they could seize power immediately; but they were equally convinced that they could not hold it against the opposition of the rest of the country. They were also aware that every major demonstration in the streets of Petersburg was now more likely than not to degenerate into street fighting. The workers were armed. Soldiers were reluctant to march in any demonstration without their rifles. Each unarmed procession offered a shooting target to the bands of the counter-revolution. The Central Committee of the Bolshevik party therefore banned all demonstrations. It was, however, unable to enforce the ban — the revolutionary temper in the suburbs and barracks had grown beyond its control. This was the background to the grave crisis of the "July days," in which Stalin played a curious role, and which ended in a severe though temporary setback for Bolshevism.

A vivid and apparently truthful account of the events was given by Stalin himself in a report to the sixth Congress of the party which met a couple of weeks after the "July days." On 3 July, in the afternoon, a delegation from one of the regiments burst into the city conference of the party and declared that their regiment and others had decided to "come out" that same evening, that they had already sent messengers to other regiments and factories calling everybody to join in the revolt. Volodarsky, the leader of the Petersburg Committee, sternly reminded the soldiers that the party expected them, as its members, to observe the ban on demonstrations. The Central Committee, the Petersburg Committee, and the Bolshevik Military

Organization then met, once again confirmed the ban, and sent agitators to the factories and barracks to enforce it there. At the same time the Central Committee delegated Stalin to inform the Executive of the Soviets, which was controlled by the Mensheviks, about the new development. Two hours after these events had begun to unfold, Stalin was carrying out his mission. But the avalanche was already on the move. Toward evening, crowds of workers and a number of regiments, fully armed and flying their colours, assembled in front of the offices of the Petersburg Committee of the party. Bolshevik speakers urged the crowd to disperse peacefully, but they were interrupted by hoots and catcalls. The raging elements of revolution struck over their heads. They then proposed that the demonstrators march towards the Tauride Palace, the seat of the Soviet, and submit their demands to the Soviet Executive. To the tune of the *Marseillaise* the procession moved on. All through the night the crowd virtually besieged the Tauride Palace, waiting in vain for an answer to their main demand that the Soviet leaders disown the Provisional Government and themselves assume power.

Mensheviks and Social Revolutionaries were biding their time, meanwhile, in the expectation that they would soon be rescued by "loyal" government troops. So far the meetings and processions were peaceful, but with every hour the excitement was boiling up to an explosion. The Minister of Agriculture, Chernov, was recognized by the crowd and "placed under arrest" by a group of thugs — only thanks to Trotsky's presence of mind and his courageous intervention was the Minister, himself an old revolutionary, saved from violence and released. Long after midnight, from the balcony of the Tauride Palace, Zinoviev tirelessly argued in his high-pitched voice with the crowd, trying to achieve the impossible: to persuade the multitude to go home and yet not to damp its revolutionary temper but, on the contrary, to keep it hot. The Bolshevik Central Committee was in permanent

session, struggling with the awkward dilemma. In the end it decided that the party should take part in the demonstration in order to lead and direct it into peaceful channels. The risk was that they would not succeed in doing so; that a battle would not be avoided; and that it might end in a major defeat that would swing the scales in favour of the counter-revolution. Defeat in such a show-down was the more probable as the Bolsheviks pulled their punches all the time. The other course of action open to them was to dissociate themselves from the demonstrators and let events run their own way. The party of the revolution, however, could not show such equanimity. The masses, left to themselves, to their own passion and impatience, were sure to walk into the trap of civil war. They would never have forgiven the Bolsheviks what would have amounted to a desertion at a time of crisis. The Bolsheviks could not afford to discredit themselves in the eyes of those very people on whose confidence and support their ultimate victory depended.

In the next few days the demonstrations, growing in size and turbulence, led to sporadic clashes and bloodshed. But the worst fears of the Bolsheviks did not materialize — the clashes did not lead to regular civil war. The whole movement spent its impetus and petered out. Almost simultaneously a counter-movement was gathering momentum. To the relief of the upper and middle classes armed groups of the right wing came into action. The Bolshevik headquarters and the offices of *Pravda* were wrecked. In the middle of all this turbulence came the news of the collapse of the Russian offensive on the front. The Bolsheviks were blamed; and a cry of vengeance went up. Agitators of the right branded Lenin and his followers as German spies. A popular newspaper published faked documents purporting to prove the charge. Government troops were engaged in punitive expeditions in the Red suburbs. Throughout the "July days" Stalin, on behalf of the Central Committee, parleyed with the Executive of the Soviets and did his best to bring unwieldy elements under control. At the outset he brought the Bolshevik decision against the demonstration to the knowledge of the Executive, only to learn later on that the decision had been reversed. He then presumably had to report the change to the Soviet leaders and explain its reasons. In the ruling circles of the Soviets, Stalin's good faith was apparently taken for granted, for later on when the Government issued writs for the arrest of most Bolshevik leaders, he, though a member of the Central Committee, was not molested. It also fell to him to carry out the final act in the winding up of this semi-insurrection, the surrender by the rebels of the powerful Peter and Paul fortress. Accompanied by a Menshevik member of the Soviet Executive, Stalin went to the fortress, which was situated on an island opposite the Bolshevik headquarters, just at the moment when those headquarters were being occupied by government troops. The garrison of the fortress consisted of fiery Kronstadt sailors, the machine-gunners who had initiated the revolt, and civilian Red Guards, all refusing to surrender and preparing for a long and bloody siege. It is easy to imagine how difficult and delicate was Stalin's mission. He was helped by official assurances that the rebels would not be penalized; but they still persistently refused to surrender. In the end Stalin shrewdly persuaded them to capitulate to the Executive of the Soviets, which sounded more honourable than a surrender to the Government. A blood-bath was avoided.

The Bolshevik setback was superficial, as events would prove. Immediately after the "July days," however, the setback was exaggerated by all parties. Most Bolshevik leaders, including Lenin, thought themselves more thoroughly defeated than they actually were. The baiting of Bolsheviks grew. Lenin and Zinoviev were indicted as spies in German pay. The moderate Socialists knew the accusation was false, but their grudge against the Bolsheviks was strong enough to prevent them from defending Lenin and his colleagues against it. Many of them suspected Lenin of having made a serious attempt, in the "July days," to seize power.

The Central Committee now discussed whether Lenin and Zinoviev should hand themselves over to the authorities or whether they should go into hiding. Lenin and Zinoviev were hesitant: they feared that to avoid trial would confirm, in the eyes of uninformed opinion, the charges levelled against them. This was at first also the view of Lunacharsky and Kamenev. Stalin, on the contrary, advised them to go into hiding. It would be folly, he said, to trust the justice of the Provisional Government. An anti-Bolshevik hysteria was being so unscrupulously whipped up that any young officer or ensign escorting the "German spies" into prison, or from prison to court, would think it an act of patriotic heroism to assassinate them on the way. Lenin still hesitated to follow Stalin's advice. Stalin then approached the Executive of the Soviets and told them that Lenin was prepared to face trial if the Executive guaranteed his life and personal safety from lawless violence. As the Mensheviks and Social Revolutionaries refused to shoulder any such responsibility, Lenin and Zinoviev finally made up their minds to go into hiding.

On 8 July Lenin disappeared, no doubt remembering the example of Robespierre who, shortly before his rise to power, was similarly hunted and found refuge with a Jacobin carpenter. Lenin's "carpenter" was the workman Alliluyev, Stalin's old friend. In his house Lenin lived for a few days. On 11 July Stalin and Alliluyev escorted Lenin through the darkening streets of the city to the Maritime Station where Lenin left to hide first in the villages near the capital and then in Finland. From now on until the October Revolution he remained underground, inspiring the strategy, if not the tactics, of his party through the pamphlets, articles, and letters which he showered on the Central Committee. Together with Lenin departed Zinoviev. A few days later Kamenev was imprisoned. So were Trotsky — after he had openly declared his solidarity with Lenin — Lunacharsky, and others. The great leaders and tribunes were dispersed. At that critical moment Stalin once again stepped to the fore to lead the party. His relative anonymity stood him in good stead; for his name did not arouse the anger and the hatred inspired by the others.

Soon after Lenin's departure he published under his full signature ("K. Stalin, member of the Central Committee," &c.) an appeal "Close the ranks," addressed to the defeated but not routed party. He repeated that in the "July days" the hands of the Bolsheviks were forced by events, that the counter-revolution had gone over to the attack, and that the "conciliators" burdened themselves with a heavy responsibility. The offensive of the counter-revolution was not yet over — "from the attack on the Bolsheviks they are now passing to an attack on all Soviet parties and the Soviets themselves." He forecast a new political crisis: "Be ready for the coming battles. . . . Our first warning is: do not lend yourselves to counter-revolutionary provocation, arm yourselves with endurance and self-control, save forces. . . . Our second warning is: draw closer around our party . . . encourage the weak, rally those who lag behind." He repeated the same instructions to the city conference of the Bolsheviks, which had begun before the "July days" and was now half-secretly resumed. The conference adopted a manifesto written by Stalin in a style that was a peculiar mixture of the revolutionary and the oriental, sacerdotal idiom:

Those gentlemen evidently hope to confound our ranks, to sow doubt and confusion amid us and to make us distrust our leaders. The wretches! They do not know that never have the names of our leaders [i.e. the names of Lenin, Trotsky, Zinoviev, Kamenev] been as dear and near to the working class as they are now when the impudent bourgeois rabble is slinging mud at them. The venal traitors!

They do not even guess that the heavier the slander of bourgeois hirelings the deeper the love of the workers for their leaders. . . . The shameful stigma of slanderers . . . take that stigma from the hands of 32 thousand organized workers of Petersburg and carry it to your grave. . . . And you, gentlemen capitalists and landlords, bankers and profiteers, priests and agents of the counter-espionage . . . you are celebrating your victory too early. You have taken too early to burying the great Russian Revolution. The Revolution is alive, and will yet let you feel it, Messieurs the grave-diggers.

The Bolsheviks, indeed, quickly recovered from the blow. By the end of July they were able to hold half-secretly a national Congress at which 240,000 members, three times as many as in April, were represented. Stalin and Bukharin were the chief spokesmen for the Central Committee. A high light of the Congress was a debate between Stalin, Bukharin, and Preobrazhensky on the character of the approaching revolution. In part the debate was an echo of the controversy over Lenin's April Theses; in part it was an anticipatory flash of a more dramatic controversy in years to come. Stalin tabled a motion to the effect that the victorious Russian Revolution would direct its power "in alliance with the revolutionary proletariat of the advanced countries toward peace and the Socialist reconstruction of society." Preobrazhensky, a young Marxist economist, tabled an amendment saying that the revolutionary government should "direct its power towards peace and — if proletarian revolution materializes in the west — towards socialism." In both versions the "alliance" between the Russian revolution and the western European proletariat was taken for granted. In Preobrazhensky's view, however, Russia could not embark upon Socialist construction unless western Europe, too, was revolutionized. Failing this, the revolution could only achieve peace (and presumably the consolidation of the democratic order). Bukharin defined the objectives of the revolution in much the same way. Stalin saw no reason why Russia could not start building socialism, regardless of whether there was a revolution in the west or not:

"You cannot rule out the possibility," so he argued against Preobrazhensky, "that precisely Russia will be the country that paves the way to Socialism. . . . The base of the revolution is broader in Russia than in western Europe, where the proletariat stands alone against the *bourgeoisie*. With us the working class is supported by the poor peasantry. . . . In Germany the apparatus of state power works with incomparably greater efficiency. . . . We ought to discard the obsolete idea that only Europe can show us the way. There exists a dogmatic Marxism and a creative one. I am opting for the latter."

Paradoxically enough, at that stage, Stalin's view appeared to be identical with Trotsky's; for Trotsky, too, argued that Russia would *begin* the Socialist revolution before Europe. Stalin did not yet expound the idea of Socialism in one country, the view that Russia by herself, in isolation from the rest of the world, could build to the end the edifice of socialism. Only seven or eight years later would he formulate that view jointly with Bukharin and against Trotsky. But already now there was a stronger emphasis in his words on Russia's peculiar Socialist mission than either in Trotsky's or in Lenin's. In Trotsky's and Lenin's writings of those days that emphasis could also be found but it was offset by their equally categorical insistence on the *ultimate* dependence of the fate of socialism in Russia on proletarian revolution in the west. Russia could and would begin the building of socialism before the other more advanced countries, but she could not carry it far all by herself — argued Lenin and Trotsky. Stalin tended to repeat the first half of the thesis but not the second. His words did in fact breathe an implicit, only half-conscious faith in Russia's revolutionary self-sufficiency. In July and August 1917 nobody was aware of these meaningful hints at future schism.

There is a touch of irony in the circumstance that at a Congress run by Stalin, Trotsky's group formally merged with the Bolshevik party and that the still-imprisoned Trotsky was elected to its new Central Committee. The other members were Lenin, Stalin, Kamenev, Zinoviev, Sverdlov, Rykov, Bukharin, Nogin, Uritsky, Miliutin, Kollontai, Artem, Krestinsky, Dzerzhinsky, Yoffe, Sokolnikov, Smilga, Bubnov, Muralov, Shaumian, Berzin. The Congress paid its homage to the persecuted leaders by electing Lenin, Trotsky, Zinoviev, Lunacharsky, Kamenev, and Kollontai to the "honorary presidium."

Meanwhile, the man who directed the party in the absence of the great ones produced no great ideas. There was no sweep of original thought in his speech. His words were dry and lacked fire. But he had the confidence of a man who had in the middle of battle stepped wittingly into a breach. His steadfastness and reliability were enough to quell any incipient panic in the ranks. While he was making his report to the Congress news was received of punitive expeditions against the Bolsheviks in various towns, including Tsaritsyn (the future Stalingrad) and of virtual martial law in various parts of the country. The Congress did not stir. Like the Koba of the old Baku days, during the ebb of the First Revolution, the Stalin of these was still able calmly to weather the storm.

After the Congress, when the imprisoned leaders, first Kamenev and then Trotsky, Lunacharsky, and others were gradually released, Stalin again withdrew into the twilight of the *coulisse*.

At the end of August the capital was alarmed by the revolt of General Kornilov, the Commander-in-Chief, against the Provisional Government, a revolt that confirmed the persistent Bolshevik warnings of an imminent counter-revolution. The origin of the *coup* was obscure. The Prime Minister Kerensky had contemplated a final show-down with the Bolsheviks and had asked General Kornilov to send reliable forces to the capital. The General was not content with the plan to suppress Bolshevism — he wanted to rid the country of the Soviets, the moderate Socialists, and Kerensky himself as well. Inflated with self-confidence and the sense of his own mission as "savior of society," he made no bones about his intentions, withdrew allegiance from the Government, and, having surrendered Riga to the Germans, ordered his troops to march on Petersburg.

The Government, the Soviets, the Menshevik and Social Revolutionary Committees and Executives were now in a panic. They were not in a position to defeat Kornilov's *coup* without help from the Bolsheviks, without arming the workers who followed Lenin, without reviving the Soviets and calling back to life the Red Guards suppressed in the "July days." Kerensky himself asked the Bolsheviks to induce the sailors of Kronstadt, who had been so active in the July mutiny, to "protect the revolution." Keeping their own grievances and resentments under control, the Bolsheviks responded to the appeal and fought "in the first ranks" against Kornilov. The counter-revolution overreached itself and drove all Socialist factions to form a "united front," which spelt its doom. The Bolsheviks, on the other hand, were careful not to commit a similar mistake. When the sailors of Krondstadt visited Trotsky in his prison and asked him whether they should not "deal" with Kornilov and Kerensky at one stroke, Trotsky advised them to tackle their adversaries one by one. After a few days the Kornilov *coup* collapsed.

The abortive counter-revolution gave Bolshevism the impetus it needed for the last lap on its road to power. The Bolsheviks emerged from the crisis with the halo of the most determined, if not the only, defenders of the revolution. When, after the suppression of Kornilov's revolt, Lenin openly called upon the Mensheviks and Social Revolutionaries to break up their partnership with the Cadets, Kornilov's accomplices, to take the reins of government into their own hands, and to base it exclu-

sively on the Soviets, promising that if his advice was followed the Bolsheviks would play the role of a legal, constitutional opposition within the framework of the Soviets; and when the Mensheviks and Social Revolutionaries rejected that advice, they irretrievably discredited themselves in the eyes of the working classes. The popularity of the Bolsheviks grew in the army together with their ever louder clamour for peace and for land for the peasants. . . .

A few days after the arrest of General Kornilov, an important event occurred in the Petersburg Soviet. As a result of recent by-elections, the Bolsheviks became the majority party. Similar shifts occurred in the Soviets of Moscow and other towns. Soon Trotsky, released on bail, was elected President of the Petersburg Soviet, the post he had held in 1905. Under his guidance the Soviet demanded from the Central Executive, still dominated by the moderate Socialists, that the second All-Russian Congress of Soviets should be called and all power transferred to it. Logically, this resolution was the prelude to insurrection. As long as Mensheviks and Social Revolutionaries were in a majority, the Bolshevik clamour "all power to the Soviets" could have no immediate practical consequences. What that slogan meant was that the Soviet majority, Mensheviks and Social Revolutionaries, should take full power. It was up to that majority to follow or not to follow that course of action. But presently "all power to the Soviets" implied power for the Bolsheviks, the new majority party. And what — the question inevitably arose — if the Provisional Government refused to yield to that demand and efface itself in favour of the Soviets? Then, the Soviets would be under the political obligation to assert their claims against the Provisional Government, to overthrow it, and to put an end to the existing dualism of power. This could be achieved only through insurrection.

THE BOLSHEVIK VICTORY: WHY DID THE PROVISIONAL GOVERNMENT FALL? AND WHY DID THE BOLSHEVIKS SUCCESSFULLY SEIZE POWER?

Both Left and Right Betrayed the Provisional Government

ALEXANDER KERENSKY

Alexander Kerensky, who was born in 1881, studied at St. Petersburg University and became a lawyer. He was a member of the Fourth Duma, and during the revolutionary events of 1917 he played a series of leading roles which are characterized in detail by several of the selections in this book. Mr. Kerensky has spent most of the years since 1917 in the United States. Always active and articulate, he has remained at the center of fierce controversies about the reasons for the Provisional Government's failures, and he has vigorously defended himself in several books. In these works, as in the article presented here, his primary purpose has been to explain his interpretation of the events.

I must here observe that that tendency to dictatorship of which I have written above, infected during the war persons who would have seemed to have been fully guaranteed against this psychosis. I quite understand the personal, human, most torturing experiences on the front, which urged Russian commanders and the officers generally into an unfortunate adventure which was hopeless from the first. But for myself even till now remain quite inexplicable the motives which induced some of the military representatives of our principal allies, both in Petersburg and at headquarters, to give active support to the general movement against that government which was directing operations important for our allies at the front. Surely by supporting the conspiracy these foreign representatives promoted a new break of discipline in the army, exactly at the time when that army was successfully completing the execution of its principal strategical task. Even if we must admit that the failure of the March Revolution heavily compromised the military position of the allies, part of the responsibility for that failure must fairly be accepted by some of their official representatives.

Now, considering the diplomatic side of the military policy of the Provisional Gov-

From Alexander Kerensky, "The Policy of the Provisional Government of 1917," *The Slavonic and East European Review*, Vol. XI, No. 31 (July, 1932), pp. 10–19. By permission of Alexander Kerensky and *The Slavonic and East European Review*.

ernment, we shall see that the task which we set ourselves, namely, the earliest conclusion of a general peace, was almost attained, and the war would not have dragged on to November 1918 if the unfortunate attempt to establish the dictatorship of General Kornilov had not opened the door to the dictatorship of Lenin.

Perhaps the unfavourable attitude towards the Provisional Government of some extremely important foreign circles of our then allies is to be explained by those new objects of the war which Russia set herself after the March Revolution, and which were only too foreign to the psychology of the time in France and England, at least for official France and England. The formula of a democratic peace, which was later developed in the famous Fourteen Points of the declaration of President Wilson, but was then for the first time proclaimed in a condensed form in the April declaration of the Provisional Government, seemed to many in the west inadmissibly doctrinaire at the time of the war and revolution and almost as criminally Germanophil.

In its solemn manifesto on the objects of the war the Provisional Government declared that, defending its frontiers, the free and democratic Russian people did not want to seize foreign territory, would not impose contributions on its enemies, and aimed at the quickest possible general and just peace on the basis of the self-determination of peoples.

Now, in 1932, for English public opinion which so clearly understands all the imperfections of the Treaty of Versailles, it is difficult to imagine with what keen apprehension and often unconcealed irritation diplomatists in 1917 received our formula of a "democratic peace." However, for the Provisional Government the formulating of new and extremely democratic war aims was not only a demand of "revolutionary idealism," but even a practical necessity; the renunciation of "imperialist war aims," the declaration of defence of one's own country as the only cause for the continua-

tion of military operations, was the obligatory first psychological condition of restoring the efficiency of the front.

Besides that, the new war diplomacy of the Provisional Government, resting on these new war aims, made it possible to prepare the exit from the war of some of the allies of Germany, particularly Bulgaria and Turkey. I have already mentioned the psychological effect which the March Revolution had on the Slavonic troops and partly on the Turkish (in consequence of the renunciation of Constantinople) in the armies of the coalition of the Central Powers. A similar favourable effect for us and our allies the March Revolution produced also on the civil population of the Slav parts of Austria, of Bulgaria and of Turkey. Therefore it is not surprising that the result of the ardent work of our Foreign Minister, M. I. Tereshchenko, together with the diplomatic representatives of the United States, which were not at war with Bulgaria and Turkey, was that both these States were quite ready to go out of the war even without the agreement of Berlin and Vienna. They were preparing to go out about November 1917. It will be understood of itself what really decisive importance would have resulted from the opening in war-time of the Dardanelles for Russia and for her allies. Now — and the whole world now knows what the Provisional Government knew then, alas! on the eve of Lenin's rising of 7 November — the world now knows, that Vienna just before the Bolshevist Revolution had definitely decided to conclude peace, even a separate peace, at whatever cost.

Thus, the new international war policy of Russia after the fall of the Monarchy was adapted to the circumstances and at any rate fully carried out the first requisites of a war-time diplomacy; it contributed to the success of the war, it brought its end nearer, and it did not weaken the efficiency of our own front.

I do not in the slightest doubt that the real history which will be written when the passions of contemporary political strife sink down and die with us — that this history will make the following conclusions: the world war would not have lasted so long if the natural post-revolution internal process of restoring the ties of State and of society in Russia had not been interrupted by a premature attempt to establish a personal dictatorship by civil war.

To prevent a civil war was the whole object of the internal policy of the Provisional Government.

As I have written above, after the collapse of the Monarchy the Provisional Government was bound in conditions of war (i) to restore, that is, from top to bottom, the administrative apparatus of the State, and (ii) to fix the foundations of a new State and social order. Two conditions, independent of any human will, excluded the application, for the attainment of the two above-named objects of internal policy, of a dictatorial or, as they liked to say at that time, of a "strong" government. First of all, for a "strong" government, in the dictatorial sense of the word, that is, for a government which did not direct and govern, but commanded and punished, it was first necessary to have in one's hands a highly-organised and accurately functioning administration and police. Such a machinery, or even the most distant suggestion of it, the Provisional Government after the collapse of the Monarchy did not possess at all. It had to be created anew with the greatest difficulties and imperfections. But till it was established, the Government had to replace police compulsion by moral conviction. We see that later on Lenin, too, for his counter-revolutionary *coup d'état*, utilised the military and administrative apparatus established by the Provisional Government, planting everywhere, among the troops, in government institutions, in the soviets, and in the town councils, his militant cells.

The second condition which decided the internal policy of the Provisional Government was the war, which by its very nature not only in Russia, which had been so extremely weakened, but even in all the other States at war demanded the very

closest and most real national unity. Such a sacred alliance of all parties and classes finally created for the needs of the war a government which by external signs was all-powerful, a kind of dictatorial government, or even a quasi-dictatorship "of a strong personality." The first of these we saw in England at the time of the War Cabinet with Lloyd George, the second in France with Clemenceau.

Finally, at the front itself there was not only a mass of more than ten million soldiers highly agitated, recognising a certain authority only of the Left socialist parties. At the front there were also thousands of officers whose efficiency it was also necessary to maintain in conditions which were for them peculiarly tragical. The enormous majority of the officers, especially of the regular officers, and especially in the Higher Command, in the main recognised the political authority of the bourgeois parties. Of these parties, that of the Cadets or Constitutional Democrats, led by Professor Milyukov, was in a kind of monopoly. This party, which up to the fall of the Monarchy had represented the liberal-radical wing of the bourgeois opposition, at the time of the March Revolution, with the disappearance of the conservative parties from the open political stage, covered the whole Right political sector.

All that has just been said fixed, I will repeat, the main lines of all the internal policy of the Provisional Government, which did not change throughout the whole time of its existence, in spite of frequent alterations in its composition. The main line of our internal policy consisted in a continuous attempt to unite all the live creative forces of the country in order (i) to re-establish the functioning of the State apparatus, (ii) to create the bases of a new post-revolutionary political and social order, and (iii) to continue the defence of the country. The only way of opposing the forces of disruption which were driving the country into the chaos of civil war, was to draw into responsible government work the leading representatives of all political

22

parties without exception, whether bourgeois or socialist, which recognised the new order and the supreme authority of the Constituent Assembly, which had to be summoned, even in spite of the war, at the earliest possible date.

It must be said that the sudden crash of the Monarchy came about so unexpectedly for the socialist parties that their leaders did not at once understand their own rôle in the new political conditions when suddenly the masses of the people — workers, peasants and soldiers — obtained an overwhelming weight in the life of the State. In the first days of the Revolution it seemed to the leaders of the Left parties that henceforward the deciding rôle in the administration of the State had passed into the hands of the Liberals and that the socialist parties ought to help the government, though not participating in it, in so far as it did not act to the disprofit of the interests of the working classes. However strange it may seem, the cause of the so-called dualism of government and soviets in the first two months of the March Revolution was exactly this failure of the socialist parties to appreciate their importance and the part that they would have to play after the Revolution. Conscientiously executing the part of a kind of responsible opposition to the government, the soviets never measured their own pressure by the weakness of resistance both of the broken administrative machinery and of the bourgeois classes, crushed by the weight of the fall of the Monarchy.

In spite of a generally-held opinion, it is precisely the strictly bourgeois original composition of the Provisional Government — where, out of eleven Ministers, I was the only representative of the non-bourgeois democracy — that was in office in the period of the greatest "weakness of authority" of that government. But besides that — and here again we have a paradox — it was just this Cabinet that carried out "by way of revolution" all the programme of those radical political and social reforms for which afterwards, at the time of the psychological preparation of General Kornilov's *coup*

d'état, the blame was thrown on Kerensky and his "having finally fallen under the power of the soviets."

As a matter of fact, it was just this first "capitalist" Cabinet of the Provisional Government which, besides a number of decrees on freedom of speech, assembly, inviolability of person, etc., worked out the great agrarian reform (the abolition of non-labouring land tenure and landed property), prepared the law on self-government of county and town councils on the basis of proportional, universal suffrage without distinction of sex, introduced workers' control into factories and workshops, gave wide powers to workers' trade unions, introduced the eight-hour working day in all government works, laid down the principles of co-operative legislation, gave soldiers all rights of citizens apart from their service in the ranks, laid down the principle of the transformation of the Empire into a federation of free peoples, drew up the principles of the electoral law for the Constituent Assembly, etc. And all this vast legislative work, which transformed the whole political and social system of Russia, the Provisional Government carried out without any pressure "from the soviet democracy." Of its own free will it realised, with great enthusiasm and full class-abnegation, the social and political ideas of the whole Russian liberation movement, liberal and revolutionary, which had had the services of many generations from the time of Novikov and Radishchev.

To tell the truth, the legislative work by way of decrees was the easiest of all for us. The hardest was the administration in the narrow sense of the word, government work which in the chaos of the revolutionary explosion demanded an extremely strong administrative and police apparatus, which it was still necessary to create. We had to create the technical machinery, and we had to establish the authority of the government. For this last task, the government had to possess the confidence of those new strata of the population which, up to the Revolution, were only an object and not a subject of power. The whole administrative apparatus was also restored in the first two months of the revolution, but more on paper than in reality. For the new government did not know how to give orders and the population did not wish to submit, often demanding for the dispositions of the government confirmation from this or that soviet.

Thus, not only the conditions of war, but also the public mood, shaken by the Revolution, demanded the presence in the Provisional Government of representatives of all parties. After some resistance, both from the Petersburg leaders of soviets and from an insignificant minority in the Provisional Government which believed in illusions of the hegemony of the bourgeoisie, and after a brief convulsion of street fighting, representatives of the soviets and socialist parties entered the government. From the middle of May and right up to the Bolshevist counter-revolution, the Provisional Government throughout remained the government of a bourgeois-socialist coalition, including representatives of all those parties which, accepting the revolution that had taken place as final, refused all forms of dictatorship, whether personal, party, or class.

A policy of national union, of softening of class antagonisms, of averting civil war, which was always possible in the first months of the Revolution, of course, excluded all that struck the chord of the need of a "strong authority." A policy of co-operation in the administration of the State by many parties with the most various programmes is, of course, as is well known in Europe, a policy of compromise. But a policy of compromise, a policy of agreements and mutual concessions, is for a government the most difficult and unpopular, for parties the most unpleasant and irritating for the self-esteem of committees, and for the country, or more properly for the wide masses of the population not always clear and intelligible.

It may be said that war conditions fixed for Russia after the Revolution a system of the formation of government, the coalition system, which is the most difficult of all. We know that even in time of peace in countries with a prolonged experience of parliamentarism, coalitions in the government delay and complicate the government work and soon alienate public opinion. The leading members of the Provisional Government who remained in it to the end — and there were only two such — very clearly saw the objectionable sides of coalition in the government in a period of revolution; but, apart from civil war and an immediate separate peace, we had no choice whatever.

Usually the history of the March Revolution is told as a continually growing collapse at the front and a continually increasing anarchy in the country. In actual fact the history of this Revolution represents a curve of slow rise and, later, sharp fall — after the revolt of General Kornilov.

Of the essence of the war policy of the Provisional Government which rested on a coalition, I have already spoken. The essence of its internal policy was not so clear, but just as definite. This is most indisputably confirmed by the actual attempt, by way of a *coup d'état*, to replace the coalition authority of the Provisional Government by the personal dictatorship of a general. As we know, this attempt took place only after the Provisional Government had suppressed the July rising of the Bolsheviks. The summer months which preceded the movement of Kornilov were the time of the greatest fall of Bolshevist influence, in the soviets, in the factories, and at the front. At the front the commanders, together with the commissaries of the War Minister, from the time of the July offensive were able to employ disciplinary measures, including the application of military force, that is, including shooting. The authority of the commanders, which had fallen after the collapse of the Monarchy almost to nil, towards the middle of the summer had been sufficiently re-established for the chiefs of the military conspiracy to feel assured that the troops would execute their orders and that the breaking up of the soviets and the overthrow of the Provisional Government

would not call forth any serious mutiny in
the ranks of the army. As we know, these
calculations proved to be extremely exaggerated; the attempted revolt of generals
again smashed all discipline in the army
and killed the authority not only of the
High Command, but of the Provisional
Government itself. But these consequences
of their "patriotic exploit," which the reck-
less generals had not foreseen, in no way
weaken my assertion: it was only when
they again felt a certain authority in their
hands that the adherents of a personal
dictatorship at the head of the army and
among the liberal and conservative politicians, decided on their unhappy adventure.
And we know it was just the same in
Germany. The famous attempt of Kapp and
Ludendorff to repeat in 1920 Kornilov's
march of 1917 also took place only after the
German democracy had conquered anarchy
on the Left, suppressed the Spartacists, and
re-established the military and administrative machinery of the State.

But apart from a proof drawn from the
other side, namely, from the attempt at a
military pronunciamento, there are also
positive evidences of the correctness of the
coalition policy of the Provisional Government. The anarchy which broke out in
March at the works and factories and
reached the greatest excesses, gradually
towards autumn died down, to break out
again with new force only before the actual
coup d'état of the Bolsheviks. In the country
districts the number of acts of violence of
the peasants on the lands of the squires was
falling. Transport was being re-established.
The food position of the towns was improv-
ing. The town and country self-government
was reviving. Towards the end of August,
in most of the towns there were already at
work town councils elected by universal
suffrage. Country self-government was being restored, though more slowly than in
the towns. The organs of local self-government based on universal suffrage were
weakening the authority of the soviets and
diminishing their part in the local life.
Izvestia itself, then the central organ of the

Congress of the Soviets (which were not
yet Bolshevist) wrote on 25 October: "The
Soviets of soldiers' and workmen's deputies
as a whole organisation of proportions all-
Russian as to the ground covered and all-
democratic as to their social composition,
are passing through an evident crisis. The
department of the central executive committee for other towns, at the time of the
highest development of soviet organisation,
reckoned 800 local soviets. Many of them
no longer exist, still more exist only on
paper. The net of soviet organisation has in
many places been broken, in others it has
weakened and in others again it has begun
to decay. The soviets were an excellent
organisation for the fight with the old
régime, but they are quite incapable of
taking on themselves the building up of a
new régime; they have no specialists, no
experience, no understanding of business,
and, finally, even no organisation."

The summons of the Constituent Assembly, fixed for the month of November,
would finally have reduced to nothing the
part of the soviets in the history of post-
revolutionary Russia. The watchword of
the Bolshevist counter-revolution, "All
power to the Soviets," already in October
appeared simply a demogogic cover for the
dictatorial plans of Lenin.

I will not here enter into a consideration
of the economic and financial policy of the
Provisional Government. At a time of war,
and even in conditions of blockade, with
profound social changes going on in the
country itself, everything in this domain
had a temporary and conditional character.
But even then there was already felt an
immediate need of a better planned direction of the whole economic life of the
country, for which there was created by us
a Higher Council of National Economy,
such as after the war also sprang up in
Germany and later in other countries, too.

In general, all that I have written on the
policy of the Provisional Government, in
the first place is far from exhausting the
whole subject and, secondly, in no way
pursues any objects of self-defence or self-

justification. Up to this time I still do not see by what other road than that of co-operation of the whole nation it was possible to try to save Russia from civil war and a separate peace "at the mortal hour of her existence," to quote once more the prophetic phrase of Prince Lvov. Even now it seems to me that the main lines of military and internal policy of the Provisional Government were correctly traced. I entirely agree that in the weakness of our personal strength and ability, we were not able to carry out this policy properly. But then, the realisation of our government programme was interrupted by those who for some reason thought that they would know better than the Provisional Government how to govern Russia. Meanwhile, at the time when the government of the March Revolution began to be attacked from the Right in the name of dictatorship, there were absolutely no objective data for reckoning the cause of the saving of Russia and the re-establishment of her internal strength as lost. We must further bear in mind that, as opposed to dictatorships of any kind, the Provisional Government did not devise its policy out of its own head, but for the whole time of its existence accurately expressed resolutions freely adopted by all parties, except the Bolsheviks, that had any weight at all in the country.

In the course of its existence of eight months, the Provisional Government lived through four Cabinet crises. Each time, all the members of the Government, without exception, declared their agreement or even their wish to leave the Cabinet, if this was desired by the parties that entered into the coalition. I personally, the member most responsible for the work of the Provisional Government, resigned, both before Korni-lov's attempt at a *coup d'état* and before the November counter-revolution. Each time I proposed to those persons and parties which considered themselves as having a better claim than ourselves to the government of the State, openly to take on themselves the responsibility for the future of the country and, according to their discretion, to form a Cabinet. Neither the politicians responsible for the tragic escapade of General Kornilov nor the adherents of a Bolshevist dictatorship decided to respond to this. They knew that all the organised and quite free public opinion of Russia was against any kind of dictatorship, against changes of the system of government till the summons of the Constituent Assembly. Only by way of conspiracy, only by way of a treacherous armed struggle was it possible to break up the Provisional Government and stop the establishment of a democratic system in Russia after the Revolution. However, apart from the path chosen by the Provisional Government, no one had any other road but the terrible road of civil war.

In October 1917, the adherents of a personal dictatorship of some or other General, after their own disaster, impatiently awaited the overthrow of the Provisional Government by Lenin. "Let the Bolsheviks only finish with them, and then we in three weeks will establish a powerful national authority." Instead of three weeks, we have the third "five years" of the dictatorship of the Bolsheviks. The experience of the Bolshevist dictatorship has lasted infinitely longer than all the dictatorships of gallant admirals and generals, whether in Siberia or in South Russia. But in both places the result for Russia was just the same.

Kerensky Betrayed Russia

LEONID I. STRAKHOVSKY

Leonid Strakhovsky, who is a Professor in the Department of Slavic Studies at the University of Toronto, has had a varied and interesting career. Born in Russia, he served in the Russian armed forces from 1916 to 1920. After emigrating to the United States he taught history at Georgetown University and the University of Maryland. More recently he has lectured at Harvard, London, Oxford, and Cambridge. He has published several historical works, including books on the Civil War in the Soviet Union and a biographical study of Tsar Alexander I. In the article presented below, Strakhovsky's strong Monarchist feelings and the evidence he has examined lead him to make very serious charges against Alexander Kerensky and to argue that there was no Kornilov revolt. As this article indicates, these issues are still very hotly debated.

RECENTLY an article by Abraham Ascher in the *Russian Review* and a chapter in a new book by Robert D. Warth have discussed extensively the most crucial period of the Russian revolution, during which the fate of Russia was decided, and the way was paved for the bolshevik seizure of power.[1] Both authors have branded General Kornilov's action early in September 1917 as a rebellion against the Provisional Government and particularly against its Prime Minister, Alexander Kerensky, and have emphasised the thesis that had it not been for this incident, "the Provisional Government would have been able to weather the revolutionary storm that was raging throughout Russia" and would have prevented the bolshevik *coup d'état* of November. Both authors want us to believe that Kornilov was the real villain. This is essentially the thesis first advanced by Kerensky himself in his book *Prelude to Bolshevism*, written in self-justification,

and since then maintained by all supporters of the Kerensky regime. Yet from the study of the evidence it would seem that the real villain was not Kornilov, but Kerensky himself, who in deliberately betraying Kornilov also betrayed Russia into the hands of the bolsheviks.

* * *

... at midnight on 5–6 August, Kornilov finally accepted the Supreme Command and left Berdichev for Mogilyov, seat of the Supreme Headquarters. Thus for a whole week the Russian army was actually without a Supreme Commander, and this crisis coincided with a crisis in the Provisional Government itself when, in the heat of the struggle for power, ministers, including Kerensky, resigned their offices in turn and then took their resignations back, so that at one time there remained only Nekrasov, the Deputy Prime Minister, to represent the Provisional Government. Finally, on 6 August, a new Provisional Government was formed, much more to the left than the previous one, with eleven out of the eighteen portfolios held by socialists. Con-

[1] Abraham Ascher, "The Kornilov Affair," *The Russian Review*, Vol. 12, No. 4 (1953); Robert D. Warth, *The Allies and the Russian Revolution* (Durham, N. C., 1954).

From Leonid I. Strakhovsky, "Was There a Kornilov Rebellion? — A Re-appraisal of the Evidence," *The Slavonic and East European Review*, Vol. XXXIII, No. 81 (June, 1955), pp. 372, 378–95. By permission of Leonid I. Strakhovsky and *The Slavonic and East European Review*.

trary to precedent, the new government
issued no joint declaration of policy, but
merely an appeal to the nation signed by
Kerensky alone. And while Kerensky spoke
of the necessity of "iron rule" and asserted
that "freedom welded by national unity
and enthusiasm cannot be defeated," he
could offer no constructive programme. In
fact he was becoming more and more a
prisoner of the Soviets, to which the socialist ministers had to report twice a week
every decision taken by the government,
even in secret sessions. Kerensky's friend
of the time, Zinaida Gippius, states plainly:
"He is afraid of them." And it was with
such a man that Kornilov had to work in
his effort to regenerate the army and to
save the nation from utter ruin.

At this juncture Ascher asks us to believe
that both Kerensky and Kornilov "wanted
to re-establish discipline in the army and
order in the country" and that "one comple-
mented the other"; that Kerensky was "a
thoroughgoing democrat," who "merely
wanted to bolster the power of the Provisional Government by gaining the adher-
ence of a 'strong' military man." But actually from that time and until the bolshevik
overthrow of his regime, Kerensky thought
of Kornilov only as a dangerous rival, because in the words of Savinkov,[2] "to him
(and that is an incontestable fact) liberty,
revolution were foremost and Russia only
second." But Warth adds that while Kornilov "was not an outspoken reactionary,
yet with a sure instinct, men of conservative sentiment — industrialists, landowners,
officers, Kadets [members of the Constitutional Democratic Party] and Allied diplo-
mats — scented the banner of counter-revolution long before the object of their atten-
tions had done so himself and flocked to
his support." But a thoughtful historian
does not think that Kornilov represented
counter-revolution when he comments: "In
the past, during the political rivalry between the Provisional Government and the
Soviets, it was possible to choose between

the tactics of the Moderate Democrats and
the Socialists, between Miliukov and
Kerensky. But the situation had under-
gone a radical change. The opposing forces
now were Lenin on the one hand and Kornilov on the other — communism versus
military dictatorship. The country had to
make a choice between the two."[3] Yet to
Kerensky, the tight-rope walker who clung
to power at all costs, even at the cost of
Russia's future, Kornilov was merely "a dangerous rival." As for the latter, he considered Kerensky more and more a tool rather
than a master. And while he was willing
to co-operate with Kerensky and his hand-
picked ministers for the best interests of
Russia, a time was to come when he would
realise that Kerensky was a puppet, whose
strings were more and more being pulled
by the Soviets with their constantly growing and overwhelmingly vociferous membership of bolsheviks.

On the basis of his agreement with Commissar Filonenko before taking up the
Supreme Command, Kornilov proceeded to
work out a programme of reforms in the
armed forces. He was visited by Savinkov
and by Tereshchenko, the Minister of Foreign Affairs, and on 10 August, the liberal
newspaper *Rech* reported: "An agreement
seems to have been reached, and the conditions laid down by Kornilov for taking command accepted." To this Kerensky retorted
through an official release of the Provisional
Government's Press Bureau: "The communications of some newspapers that the
conditions laid down by General Kornilov
have been accepted by the Provisional
Government do not conform to reality, but
at any rate an understanding between the
Provisional Government and General Kornilov has been reached." Indeed, General
Kornilov believed that an understanding
had been reached and so he came to Petrograd on 16 August in order to present his
report and to press for its acceptance. But
the measures proposed by Kornilov were
anathema to the Soviets and hence to

[2] Boris Savinkov, member of the Socialist Revolutionary Party and former terrorist. [Editor's note]

[3] George Vernadsky, *A History of Russia* (New
Haven, 1929), p. 243.

Kerensky, who passed the report on to Savinkov and Filonenko, for revision. Thus Kornilov reported only on the general military situation, painting a gloomy picture and warning of a possible enemy offensive on the Riga front. He concluded: "Although counter-measures have been taken, it is unlikely that, in view of the general instability of the armed forces and particularly of the army on the north-western front, we could stop the enemy's advance."

It was during this report to the full membership of the Provisional Government that a significant incident occurred. In his later testimony before the Investigating Committee Kornilov stated:

When I broached the subject of a possible offensive on a certain sector of the front, provided certain conditions were met, the prime minister, who sat next to me, bent over and whispered that I should be careful about what I was saying. This warning was provoked by a note handed to Kerensky by Savinkov and Tereshchenko which said: "Is the prime minister sure that the Russian and Allied state secrets being revealed by General Kornilov will not become known to the enemy through *comradely* channels?" I was stunned and deeply disturbed by the realisation that in the Council of Ministers of the Russian State the Supreme Commander could not without apprehension touch upon such matters which he considers necessary to lay before the government in the interests of national defence. At the end of the meeting it became clear to me from certain remarks made by Savinkov that the warning had in view Chernov, the Minister of Agriculture.

Ascher, following Kerensky's own lead, treats this incident lightly, but one can imagine the shock which the stalwart soldier experienced when he realised that there were potential traitors among Kerensky's cabinet ministers. No wonder that his distrust of this Second Coalition Provisional Government grew steadily as time went on, and he found no co-operation from this government for the enactment of measures which he rightly considered not only as necessary but essential for the salvation of Russia.

Before leaving the capital at 3 a.m. on 17 August, Kornilov gave an interview to the press. *Rech* reported: "General Kornilov proposed certain measures for the improvement of conditions in the army. He is convinced, and feels that the Provisional Government is of the same mind, that without these measures, the enactment of which he expects in the next few days, it is impossible to restore the fighting ability of the army. It is very necessary that the Provisional Government should adopt these measures." But *Izvestiya*, the organ of the Soviets, commented: "The demands of General Kornilov, in the form of an ultimatum, supported by the possibility of a new attack by the enemy, put the Provisional Government in a very difficult position, and the future alone knows how it will act. This, however, may be said at present: the sympathies of the democracy [i.e. the Soviets] are not on the side of General Kornilov." From this moment on the leftist press, taking a cue from *Izvestiya*, started an energetic campaign against Kornilov. This in turn led to the passing of resolutions by the Council of the Union of Cossack Troops on 19 August, by the Union of Officers of the Army and Navy on 20 August, and by the Union of the Knights of St. George on 21 August, vigorously supporting the Supreme Commander.

Meanwhile Kerensky stubbornly refused all Savinkov's entreaties even to read the text of Kornilov's proposed measures as revised by Savinkov and Filonenko. Finally, on 21 August, he informed Savinkov bluntly that under no circumstances would he sign such a document. This was Kerensky's fatal mistake. But Ascher exonerates him: "Indeed, in the light of the existing political situation it was most difficult for him to do so. It would most probably have meant the alienation of groups whose support he desperately needed." Indeed, Kerensky needed the support of the Soviets to maintain himself in power, but in relying on it he not only prepared his own downfall, but the collapse of Russia as well.

Exasperated by Kerensky's stubbornness and lack of unselfish statesmanship, Savinkov tendered his resignation as Deputy Minister of War. But Kerensky refused to accept it. Then Savinkov learned that Kornilov had decided not to come to Petrograd for another effort to get his proposed and revised measures enacted, as had been agreed at the end of his first visit, because of intelligence which had reached him that an attempt on his life was being prepared in the capital. In desperation Savinkov and Filonenko called Kornilov by telegraph on 22 August. "Your presence here tomorrow is absolutely essential," pleaded Savinkov; "without your help I shall not be able to defend what both you and I consider right." To this Filonenko added that he and Savinkov had planned to give "general battle" the next day in order to change the government's policy in line with Kornilov's programme. Finally Kornilov yielded to the arguments of these two political friends, who were to desert him, nevertheless, at the crucial hour. But he took precautions and came to Petrograd on 23 August accompanied by a squadron of the Tekinsky Cavalry Regiment armed with machine guns.

Contrary to Mr. Ascher's statement, it was not Kornilov who was afraid of Kerensky, but Kerensky of Kornilov. Having learned of Savinkov's démarche in urging Kornilov's visit to Petrograd, Kerensky, without informing Savinkov, had dispatched the following telegram to the Supreme Commander: "The Provisional Government did not call for you, nor did it insist on your arrival and therefore does not assume any responsibility in this matter, in view of the existing strategic conditions." But this telegram reached Kornilov only when he had already arrived in the capital, and it is doubtful whether it would have stopped him.

Kornilov was met at the station by Savinkov and Filonenko, who handed to him the revised copy of his original report which they had both signed. From the station Kornilov went directly to Kerensky's apartment in the Winter Palace. It is difficult to ascertain what happened at this meeting because of the opposing evidence of Kornilov and Kerensky, but one thing is certain, namely that Kerensky won a tactical victory when he prevented Kornilov's report, modified by Savinkov and Filonenko, from being discussed by the full membership of the Provisional Government on the ground that he himself had had no time yet to study it. Nevertheless, the report, to which Kornilov had also affixed his signature, was read and discussed by Kornilov that evening at a private meeting with Kerensky, Nekrasov and Tereshchenko, at which it was strongly argued against by the latter two while Kerensky kept silent. While this meeting was taking place, Savinkov read Kornilov's report to his friends, the Merezhkovskys. Here is how Zinaida Gippius recorded it in her diary:

Savinkov read it to us in its entirety, beginning with a most detailed and all-embracing analysis of the situation at the front (it is most shocking even on the surface!) and ending by a similarly concise exposition of those immediate measures which have to be enacted both at the front and in the rear. This very lengthy report, in which every word has been thought out and weighed, will some time find its commentator — at any rate it will not be lost. I shall say only what is most important: it is undoubtedly that minimum which as yet might save the honour of the revolution and the life of Russia in her present unheard-of situation.

I think that, indeed, there will still be bargaining with Kerensky. But it seems that even in all its details it is a minimum, including the militarisation of the railways and the death penalty in the rear. I can imagine how the "comrades" will howl! (And Kerensky is afraid of them, this must be remembered.)

They will howl, because they will discover in this a fight against the Soviets — that hideous abnormally developed phenomenon, that breeding place of bolshevism, a phenomenon before which even now the democratic leaders and sub-leaders, non-bolsheviks, reverently bow. It is some kind of immutably stupid criminality!

They will be right: it is a fight against the Soviets, although openly nothing is said in the report about the destruction of the Soviets. On the contrary, Boris [Savinkov] added even that "it is necessary to retain the soldiers' committees, because one cannot do without them." But no committee of any sort should be permitted to interfere in matters of command.

And still it is (at last!) a fight against the Soviets.

And Kerensky must have understood that the report meant exactly what Zinaida Gippius surmised — a fight against the Soviets. But he was not only afraid of them, he had to rely on their vacillating support to remain in power, which was more important to him than the fate of Russia. And Kornilov must have been aware by this time that Kerensky was too weak to head a "strong" government, because he would never dare to challenge the vicious authority of the Soviets. It was then that he decided to appeal directly to the nation in an attempt to arouse the sane, vital, patriotic and honourable sentiments still alive in the country. This he was to do at the Moscow Conference, an unwieldy heterogeneous gathering of over twenty-five hundred delegates supposedly representative of the nation as a whole, which the Provisional Government had called for 25 August.

In the meantime another attempt to force Kerensky's hand was made when in the morning of 24 August Kokoshkin, a leading member of the Constitutional Democratic Party, who held the office of State-Comptroller in the Provisional Government, threatened to resign from the government, if Kornilov's programme was not adopted forthwith. In order to appease Kokoshkin and the other members of his party who held cabinet posts, Kerensky informed the members of his government for the first time at a meeting that day of the contents of Kornilov's report, but only in its first version and revealing only the portions dealing directly with military affairs. After a heated discussion a compromise was reached, accepting Kornilov's programme in principle — another fine example of Kerensky's prevarication.

"The Moscow State Conference opened in an atmosphere charged with alarm and nervous expectation," reported *Rech*. The membership was about equally divided between the socialist and non-socialist groups. And Kerensky attempted to steer a middle course, throwing threats to the right and to the left alike, whereas "on the left there was the real and growing danger of bolshevism and on the right only the spurious and problematic menace of 'counter-revolution' and military dictatorship."[4] Zinaida Gippius commented bitterly on Kerensky's behavior at the Conference:

He is like a railway carriage that has left the rails. He sways, vacillates painfully and — without any glamour. . . . I loved him as he was before (and do not deny it); I understand his difficult position; I remember how during the first days he *took an oath* before the Soviets always to remain with the *democracy*, how with one stroke of the pen he abolished the death penalty *forever*. . . . And now if he were to join Kornilov and Savinkov it would be a betrayal of the *oath to the Soviets*, and the *death penalty* again. . . . But still there are only two honourable ways for Kerensky, only two. Either to go along with Kornilov, Savinkov and the famous programme, or to declare quietly and openly: this is what is needed at this critical moment, but I cannot do it and hence I am leaving. . . . But he is seeking a third way, wants to hold back something, to put putty in the ominous crack, to prolong the lingering. . . . But there is no third way, and Kerensky will find himself without a way, he will meet an inglorious end. . . . and it is good, if it is his end alone.

And Kerensky did exactly this. He did not heed the warning of General Kornilov, delivered at the Moscow Conference on 27 August, when the Supreme Commander said:

It is with deep sorrow that I must declare openly that I have no certainty that the Russian army would fulfill unflinchingly its duty to the fatherland. . . . The shame of the Tarnopol disaster is the direct and inevitable consequence of that unheard-of ruin which befell

4 Michael T. Florinsky, *Russia: A History and an Interpretation* (New York, 1953), II, 1434.

our army, once glorious and victorious, as the result of influences from outside and of careless measures adopted for its reorganization. . . . The enemy is already pounding at the gates of Riga and if the instability of our army will not give us a possibility to hold on to the shore of the Riga Gulf, the road to Petrograd will be open to invasion. . . . I have faith that the fighting qualities of our army and her former glory will be restored. But I declare that *there is no time to lose,* that one should not waste *a single minute.* We need determination and the firm unflinching carrying out of proposed measures. . . . The army must be revived at all costs, for without a strong army there can be no free Russia and no salvation of the country. In order to revive the army, it is necessary to accept at once and *without delay* (Kornilov repeated this twice) the recommendations which I have made to the Provisional Government. My report was countersigned, without any reservations whatsoever, by the Deputy Minister of War, Savinkov, and Commissar Filonenko, attached to Supreme Headquarters. . . . It is inconceivable to admit that determination should manifest itself each time only under the pressure of defeats and loss of territory. If stern measures for the restoration of discipline at the front were introduced as the result of the Tarnopol disaster and the loss of Galicia and Bukovina, *one should not permit that the establishment of order in the rear* would be the consequence of our loss of Riga or that order on the railways should be restored at the price of ceding to the enemy Moldavia and Bessarabia.

The impression made by Kornilov's speech was immense and deeply depressing. This time he gave a warning and appealed not only to the government, but to the nation at large. But the government, personified by Kerensky, who was "its head, its inspiration, and its symbol,"[5] now saw in Kornilov not merely a dangerous rival, but the leader of a counter-revolutionary plot. As to the nation it was now more divided than ever. The so-called "democratic forces," i.e. the socialists of various hues, including the bolsheviks, were more concerned with what they called "the gains

of the revolution" than with the future of Russia and, while ostensibly supporting Kerensky, actually drove him further and further into the abyss. Whereas all the sane and vital elements of the country now looked toward Kornilov as their only hope to save Russia from oblivion. And coming events seemed to play into the General's hand.

On 31 August the Germans started their offensive against Riga, as Kornilov had warned, and three days later, on 3 September, notwithstanding feverish efforts of the Supreme Command, which were nullified by the refusal of soldiers to fight, the city was captured by the enemy with little effort. And as Kornilov predicted, this new disaster stirred the government into action. It was decided to send to the front all those regiments stationed in the capital which had participated in the July uprising and to replace them by more reliable units, particularly cavalry regiments, which had already been arriving in Petrograd on their way to Finland. At the same time Savinkov, who had just been appointed also Deputy Minister of the Navy, was sent to Supreme Headquarters on 4 September to confer with Kornilov. There, on 6 September, he informed the Supreme Commander that the latter's proposed measures would be enacted in a few days; that a bolshevik uprising was expected about 9–10 September and that the publication of Kornilov's programme would provide them with a new stimulus to action; that the reaction of the socialist-revolutionaries and of the mensheviks was uncertain and hence the government could not rely on the garrison. "Therefore," he said, "I ask you to issue orders that the Third Cavalry Corps should be concentrated in the vicinity of Petrograd and be placed at the disposal of the Provisional Government. In case, besides the bolsheviks, the members of the Soviet of Workers' and Soldiers' Deputies also rise against the government, we shall have to apply decisive and merciless measures against them as well." It was then also agreed that Kornilov should inform Savinkov by telegraph of the

5 Florinsky, *Russia,* p. 1434.

exact time when the Third Cavalry Corps would approach Petrograd so that the Provisional Government would know when to proclaim the capital under martial law. Thus the concentration of the Third Cavalry Corps in the vicinity of Petrograd, a measure which was later claimed by Kerensky and Savinkov and their apologists as the first step of the Kornilov rebellion, was carried out at the specific demand of Savinkov who, supposedly, was following Kerensky's instructions.

At this juncture an important question arises: was Kerensky straightforward in his dealings with Kornilov or was he trying to set a trap for the Supreme Commander and the "counter-revolutionary conspiracy," which he was ferreting out ever since the Moscow Conference? In the opinion of Milyukov, Gippius, and Florinsky all the evidence points strongly to the fact that Kerensky betrayed Kornilov. And the episode of V. N. L'vov, who took upon himself the task of reconciling the opposing attitudes of Kerensky and Kornilov by acting as go-between, of which both Ascher and Warth make a great deal, only played into Kerensky's hands. Professor Vernadsky sums up the situation very aptly in these words:

Kornilov's plan of reinstating discipline in the army was based upon the co-operation of the Provisional Government. If he had had to deal with the first Provisional Government, headed by Prince Lvov, it is quite likely that his plan of subjecting the government to his will would have succeeded. But unluckily for him, the head of the government was no longer Prince Lvov, but Kerensky, who was not sufficiently strong to retain power for himself, but who had enough political cunning to prevent anyone else from taking it from him so long as the Provisional Government continued to exist.[6]

The crisis came to a head with the so-called "mission" of V. N. L'vov. A constitutional democrat, member of the last Duma and former Procurator of the Holy Synod

[6] Vernadsky, *A History*, p. 243.

in the first Provisional Government, L'vov visited Kerensky at the Winter Palace on 4 September and urged him to reorganise his government on a broader basis to include even moderate monarchists. According to L'vov's statement to the Investigating Committee, Kerensky showed perfect willingness to follow L'vov's advice, even stating that he was ready to step down from the office of Prime Minister. Thus L'vov felt not only encouraged by this interview, but even that he was entrusted by Kerensky to negotiate for the formation of a new government. Actually Kerensky wanted to use L'vov in order to ferret out the "counter-revolutionary" plot which had become his obsession since the Moscow Conference.

The next day L'vov left Petrograd on his "mission." After stopping in Moscow, where he had interviews with conservative political leaders, L'vov proceeded to Mogilyov where he had two meetings with Kornilov on 6 and 7 September. He assured the Supreme Commander that he had been entrusted by Kerensky, "who does not cling to power and is willing to resign if he were in the way," to find out Kornilov's views on a reorganisation of the government. Kornilov stated bluntly that in view of the critical situation both at the front and in the rear he could not see any way out of the dilemma except through the establishment of a dictatorship and the placing of the entire country under military law. "I declared," he testified later, "that I have no personal aspirations to power and that I am ready to submit immediately to the one who is invested with dictatorial powers, whether it is Kerensky himself or some other person." At the same time he announced that if dictatorial powers were conferred upon him by the Provisional Government, he would not refuse to do his duty.

But when L'vov reported to Kerensky on 8 September, Kornilov's suggestions were presented as demands. Kerensky seized upon this ultimative nature of Kornilov's proposal as reported by L'vov to proclaim it to be a plot against his regime. He even went so far as to impersonate L'vov, already under arrest, in an exchange of messages by telegraph with Kornilov in order to obtain confirmation of the would-be conspiracy. Yet a careful scrutiny of the text of these messages does not reveal any plot on the part of Kornilov, who pursued the much discussed idea of the formation of a strong government either with himself or some other strong personality at the head of it, and with the participation of Kerensky. Even at this stage Kornilov trusted Kerensky. "Although he did not believe that Kerensky would dare to undertake an open struggle against the Soviet, he believed fully that Kerensky, like himself, was inspired not by a personal taste for power but by the welfare of the country. He did not expect that at the last minute Kerensky would stubbornly cling to power in a desire to hold to it at all costs, even at the risk of jeopardising what, in Kornilov's opinion, was the last chance to save the Russian state."[7]

After the exchange of messages with Kornilov, which ended with Kerensky's promise to visit Supreme Headquarters the next day, ostensibly to come to an agreement with the Supreme Commander, the Prime Minister announced to his astounded cabinet members that he had discovered Kornilov's plot against the government and demanded unlimited powers to deal with the situation as well as to reorganise the government. Whereupon all fourteen cabinet ministers handed him their resignations. From then on and until a new government was formed, there were no more cabinet meetings, and Kerensky acted dictatorially.

Kerensky's first act was to send a telegram in his own name and without an official number dismissing Kornilov from the Supreme Command and demanding his presence in Petrograd. This came as a thunderbolt to Kornilov, who was expecting Kerensky's and Savinkov's arrival that very day. Before receiving the order of his dismissal, Kornilov, in fulfilment of his

agreement with Savinkov, sent him the following telegram, dated 9 September at 2:40 p.m. — "The corps will be concentrated in the vicinity of Petrograd towards the evening of 10 September. I request proclamation of martial law in Petrograd on 11 September. No. 6394. General Kornilov. Countersigned: Lukomsky, Romanovsky." Was that the act of a plotter and would-be rebel — to inform the opponent of his plans and troop concentrations? It was natural, then, for Kornilov to assume, upon receipt of Kerensky's personal telegram announcing his dismissal that the Prime Minister had fallen completely under the influence of the Soviets and was acting on his own and not as the head of the Provisional Government. Hence Kornilov refused to surrender his command. It was obviously an act of insubordination, but certainly not of mutiny or rebellion as Kerensky wanted it to appear.

From the beginning of the crisis Savinkov believed that it was a misunderstanding and wanted to get in touch with Kornilov the very evening of 8 September, when Kerensky informed the cabinet of the Supreme Commander's "rebellion," but was prevented from doing so by Kerensky. Yet the very next day, 9 September, Savinkov gave an interview to the press in which he declared that "General Kornilov enjoys the absolute confidence of the Provisional Government," that his proposals have been "accepted" and that "the measures of the Supreme Commander for the improvement of the front and of the rear and for the restoration of discipline in the army are supported by the Provisional Government which will not delay enacting them." But at the same time Kerensky revealed at a conference with some former members of his cabinet the text of a declaration in which, distorting the facts completely, he declared that General Kornilov had sent V. N. L'vov, member of the State Duma, to him

---

[7] P. N. Milyukov, *Istoriya vtoroy russkoy revolyutsii* (Sofia, 1921), I, 181–82.

with a *demand* that the Provisional Government hand over to General Kornilov all civil and military powers so that he may, according to his own judgment, form a new government. The fact of the authorization of V. N. L'vov was confirmed by General Kornilov in a conversation *with me* by direct wire. *Having concluded* that the presentation of these demands expresses the desire of certain circles of the Russian public to take advantage of the difficult situation in the State for *the reestablishment in the country of a regime opposed to the conquests of the revolution,* the Provisional Government has found it necessary in order to save the fatherland, liberty and the *republican* form of government to authorise me to take quick and decisive measures so as to cut at the roots all attempts *to challenge the supreme authority* in the State and *the rights of citizens won by the revolution.*[8]

This was an accusation of General Kornilov as a counter-revolutionary who desired to re-establish the monarchy, which was blatantly untrue. As to the republican form of government, it was still an open question since it was up to the Constituent Assembly to decide it. As Zinaida Gippius noted in her diary: "It was obvious from the beginning that the ulcer of enmity had burst in Kerensky towards Kornilov (*not* the reverse). That the attacking party is Kerensky and not Kornilov. And that for the present the winning side will be Kerensky and not Kornilov, who did not expect this direct blow."

Among the ministers who attended the conference with Kerensky there was still a feeling that the whole thing was a misunderstanding, and they suggested that before the declaration was made public, the Prime Minister should contact Supreme Headquarters. This Kerensky accepted and the conference adjourned at 1 p.m. But it was Savinkov who was delegated to try to clear the misunderstanding. And Savinkov, who had been refused this opportunity by Kerensky the night before, was eager to do so, because he must have felt that his own political reputation and integrity were in jeopardy, since he knew that the movement of the Third Corps towards Petrograd was

8 Author's italics.

undertaken upon his order and in the name of Kerensky.

When contact was established with Kornilov by telegraph, Savinkov urged Kornilov to obey the order of the Provisional Government, to surrender his command and to leave Supreme Headquarters. After referring to new alarming news — which had to deal with the German preparations to make a landing on the shores of the Gulf of Riga; with the murder of a divisional commander and of an army commissar by soldiers; and with the appalling results of the explosion in the ammunition depot in Kazan', the work of German agents — Kornilov reiterated that he had sent no ultimatums to Kerensky; that he had received V. N. L'vov as an emissary of the Prime Minister who came to offer to Kornilov a choice of three ways to reorganise the government, and that he had chosen the principle of a military dictatorship in the firm belief that there was no other way to save the country from imminent catastrophe; that he considered the participation of both Kerensky and Savinkov in the new government as essential, and that in view of the forthcoming bolshevik uprising in Petrograd he had been and was still urging both Kerensky and Savinkov to come to Supreme Headquarters, because their presence in the capital was wrought with danger for both of them, while he guaranteed their safety on his word of honour. He spoke further of his great surprise in receiving the order of his dismissal at the time when he was expecting Kerensky's arrival as promised by the latter the day before. Then he concluded: "I am deeply convinced that the completely unexpected decision of the government was undertaken under pressure of certain definite organisations. To leave my post under the pressure of these people I consider equal to desertion in the face of the enemy. Therefore, fully conscious of my responsibility before the nation, before history and before my conscience, I firmly declare that in this terrible hour in the life of the fatherland I shall not leave my post." As Zinaida

Gippius comments: *"There was no Kornilov rebellion."* And Savinkov and half a dozen officials who were with him during this conversation must have felt so, since even before the end of it Savinkov dispatched an aide to Kerensky with a request to hold up the issue of the Prime Minister's denunciation of Kornilov. But it was too late: Kerensky had broken his promise given at the conference with his former ministers and, even before the beginning of the conversation between Savinkov and Kornilov, had not only issued his declaration but had ordered resistance to the advancing Third Corps.

The fat was in the fire, and Kerensky was obviously the culprit, but he even made the pretence of stopping the publication of the government declaration, which was rather childish, since not only the text of it had been telegraphed to Supreme Headquarters but by his orders railway lines were being dismantled and fortified posts erected to stop the progress of the "rebellious" Third Corps.

Milyukov, the historian and politician, comments: "Did Kerensky understand at this moment that, by declaring himself an opponent of Kornilov, he was delivering himself and Russia into the hands of Lenin? Did he understand that this moment was the last one when the struggle against the bolsheviks could have been won by the government? But to understand this, one had to relinquish a great deal. The tragedy of Kerensky was that, although he had by now understood a great deal, he was not willing to relinquish anything. . . . If one could pin on one chronological point Kerensky's *crime* against Russia, about which so much has been said, then that *crime* was committed at that moment."[9]

Up to 10 September the public in general was not aware of the crisis, except for rumours about it in the capital, beginning as early as 8 September, which were fanned by the socialist ministers, who were also members of the Petrograd Soviet, as re-

corded in Zinaida Gippius's diary. But the storm broke with the publication all over Russia of Kerensky's indictment of Kornilov as head of a mutiny against the Provisional Government, accompanied by an order to surrender his command to General Klembovsky, commander of the northern front (which defended Petrograd) and the countercharge of the Supreme Commander, in which he called Kerensky's statement a lie, branded the whole move as a betrayal, and appealed to the nation in the name of God and of the Holy Orthodox Church to rally to the salvation of the fatherland. Kerensky opened the arsenals to arm the workers of Petrograd, who became later the nucleus of the bolshevik Red Guard, since they never surrendered their arms, but used them effectively against Kerensky's government on 7 November. The troops of the garrison started lustily to dismantle the rails ("it was not the Germans to face, there was no fear" as Zinaida Gippius commented), while the Soviet and its affiliated body, the Railway Union, mobilised their forces and sent trained propagandists to win the men of the Third Cavalry Corps to their side. At this moment Kornilov issued a stirring appeal to the nation and to the Provisional Government, which is worth quoting in full, since neither Kerensky nor his apologists have seen fit even to mention it:

I, General Kornilov, Supreme Commander of the Russian Armed Forces, declare, before the whole nation, that my duty as a soldier, my feelings as a self-denying citizen of Free Russia, and my boundless love for my country, oblige me, at this critical hour of Russia's existence to disobey the orders of the Provisional Government and to retain the Supreme Command over the Army and Navy. Supported in this decision by all the Commanders-in-Chief of the Fronts, I declare to the whole of the Russian people that I prefer to die rather than give up my post as Supreme Commander. A true son of Russia remains at his post to the end and is always ready to make the greatest of all sacrifices for his country — that of his life.

In these truly terrible moments of our country's existence, when the approaches to both capitals are almost open to the victorious advance of the triumphant foe, the Provisional Government, forgetting the great and essential question of the very independence of Russia, frightens the Russian people with the phantom of counter-revolution, which it is calling forth by its inability to direct the affairs of the country, by the weakness of its authority and its indecision.

It is not for me — a son of the people — who has given myself up, heart and soul, to the services of that people, to go against the great liberties and the great future of Russia. But at the present this future is in weak and impotent hands. The arrogant foe, by using bribery, corruption and treachery, has made himself master here as if he were at home, and threatens not only the liberties, but the very existence, of the Russian nation. Come back to your senses, O sons of Russia, recover from your madness and see the abyss into which our country is rushing blindly!

Desirous to avoid all strife, to forestall all shedding of Russian blood in civil war and forgetting all insults and injuries, I, before the whole nation as witness, appeal to the Provisional Government: "Come to Supreme Headquarters, where your freedom and safety are guaranteed on my word of honour, and together we will work out and form such a government of national defence as will make secure the liberties of the people and lead Russia to a great future, worthy of a free and mighty nation."

Kerensky's answer to this was to order the arrest of General Kornilov. Meanwhile the "defence" of the capital was taken over by the Petrograd Soviet, which formed the "Committee of People's Struggle against Counter-Revolution." Although the bolsheviks were in a minority in this committee, it is symptomatic that the report of the committee's activity to the Soviet was made by a bolshevik deputy. It was made by Bogdanov on 13 September, and said in part:

When the Provisional Government began to waver and it was not clear how the Kornilov adventure would end, there appeared would-be intermediaries, such as Milyukov and General Alekseyev, *who could have spoiled the whole business.* Then the Political Section of the Committee [of which Bogdanov was a member] came forward and with all its energy *prevented* any possible *conciliation* between the government and Kornilov. We declared that there could be no hesitation, that the government has but one way before it — that of a merciless struggle against Kornilov. *Under our influence* the government stopped all negotiations and refused to accept any of Kornilov's offers.... As to the defence of Petrograd, here too *we* had taken all necessary measures.... *During these three days we have committed many unlawful acts.* Since the Provisional Government could not take care of everything, it had asked us to inform it of the *evidence* in our possession. But *in order to obtain such evidence* it was often necessary to have recourse to decisive action. In this case we considered it our duty to help the government *regardless of the illegal aspect of our action. We decreed* the closing of four newspapers [guilty of having published Kornilov's appeal], *we carried out* searches and arrests ... *we confiscated* all arms found in the possession of unauthorised persons [including the Polish National Committee!].[10]

Need one emphasise after this that the Soviet had usurped the authority of the government? The day before this report was made Savinkov, who had been appointed Governor-General of Petrograd on 9 September, was dismissed from all his posts by Kerensky in an unprecedented way — by telephone. 'My dismissal," Savinkov related, "was demanded by the Soviet of Workers' and Soldiers' Deputies." A few days later Savinkov was even deprived of membership in the Socialist-Revolutionary Party. Obviously, the Soviet did not forgive him his earlier support of General Kornilov.

As to the troops of the Third Cavalry Corps, they stopped their bellicose advance when informed that there was no bolshevik uprising and fraternised with the propagandists of the Soviet and the "defenders" of Petrograd. Hence there was no bloodshed. Naïvely Mr. Ascher comments: "Kornilov's whole plot melted away," and Mr. Warth adds: "The organisation and planning of the *coup* was so inept as to

10 Author's italics.

endanger the whole enterprise." But it seems clear from the whole story that there was no "plot," no "mutiny," no "rebellion." Kornilov tried, as it proved against insurmountable odds, to save the country from the abyss into which it was being pushed by bolsheviks, mensheviks, and left-wing socialist-revolutionaries alike, not *against* Kerensky, but *with* Kerensky. He defied Kerensky's order of dismissal, because it was by now an established fact that Kerensky had betrayed him and given himself into the hands of the Petrograd Soviet. "Kerensky may have thought," comments a distinguished soldier, Lord Ironside, "that a Military Dictatorship was an impossible solution to the difficulties of his Government, but by destroying the Commander who might have helped him he allowed a free reign to the bolsheviks, who were preparing a Dictatorship which was to destroy him." To this may be added even a stronger indictment from the pen of Professor Milyukov: "A taste for power took precedence of actions which were imperatively dictated by the interests of Russia." But the most devastating appraisal, yet one which is most to the point, of Kerensky's role in this fatal hour of Russia's history is given by his former friend and admirer, Zinaida Gippius, who wrote in her diary on 21 October 1917:

When history changes its perspectives, someone will perhaps try again to place a hero's crown on Kerensky's head. Then my voice should also be taken into account. I do not speak personally. And I know how to observe a contemporary from afar, without emotion. Kerensky *was* what he had been at the beginning of the revolution. But Kerensky now is a cowardly and irresponsible person; and since in fact he stood on top then he alone is guilty of Russia's fall to the bottom of a bloody pit. He alone. Let people remember this.

And since concerted efforts are being made "to place a hero's crown on Kerensky's head," let the facts in this case speak out the truth, and let history pronounce its verdict of guilty in betraying Russia against the former Prime Minister of the Provisional Government, to whom the dubious gains of the March revolution were dearer than the welfare, the future, and the very existence of his country and its people.

Bolshevik Organization and Strategy Brought Victory

MERLE FAINSOD

Merle Fainsod, one of America's most distinguished political scientists, is Professor of Government and Member of the Faculty of the Graduate School of Public Administration at Harvard University. His judicial analyses of the organization of power in the Soviet Union are based upon great knowledge and painstaking research. His most recent book, *Smolensk under Soviet Rule*, is a careful study of materials captured by the Germans during World War II. In the excerpt used here, Fainsod presents the interpretation of the reasons for Lenin's success that is most widely held by expert opinion in this country.

THE medium through which the Bolsheviks organized their forces for the final coup was the Military Revolutionary Committee of the Petrograd Soviet. With the Bolsheviks in full control of the Soviet, a resolution to create the committee was carried on October 29, and the committee itself was named on November 2, four days before the insurrection. The staff of the committee was composed only of Bolsheviks and sympathetic Left SR's. Trotsky, the President of the Soviet, also served as chairman of the committee and surrounded himself with a core of reliable Bolsheviks who, in effect, comprised the general staff of the insurrection. Liaison with the Bolshevik Central Committee was maintained through a secret "military revolutionary center," consisting of five members of the committee, Sverdlov, Stalin, Bubnov, Uritsky, and Dzerzhinsky.

The party's role in directing the insurrection was camouflaged behind the façade of the Soviet. This shrewd stratagem provided a measure of pseudo-legality for the organizers of the insurrection. It was of particular value in mobilizing the support of the wavering and hesitant who were ready to respond to an appeal of the Soviet when they would have been unwilling to follow the naked leadership of the Bolsheviks. It was of outstanding importance in dealing with the Petrograd garrison which early in the Revolution had formed the habit of looking to the Soviet as its protector against transfer to the front and refused to take orders not countersigned by that body.

In its preparations for the insurrection, the Military Revolutionary Committee relied heavily on the Bolsheviks' Military Organization, which counted approximately a thousand members in the Petrograd area — among them a number of young officers as well as others with military experience. Through this organization, commissars were assigned "for observation and leadership" to the garrison's combat units, as well as to arsenals, warehouses, and other institutions of military importance. Arrangements were made through the commissars, who were in charge of issuing arms, to prevent the arming of the *Junkers*, or cadets in the military schools, and at the same time to divert rifles and other equipment to the Red Guard. Kernels of resistance developed. The Bolshevik commissar was unable to establish his authority in the important Fortress of Peter and Paul which commanded the Winter Palace. On the afternoon of

November 5, this obstacle was overcome when Trotsky appealed to the soldiers of the fortress. With this peaceful surrender went a prize of one hundred thousand rifles, no mean contribution to future success.

On the evening of the fifth, the Provisional Government made a belated attempt to fight back. The decision was made to close the Bolshevik newspapers, *Rabochii Put'* and *Soldat* (Soldier), to initiate criminal proceedings against the members of the Military Revolutionary Committee, to arrest leading Bolsheviks, and to summon reliable military units from the environs of Petrograd. The first tests of strength augured badly for the government. The Bolshevik printing plants were raided by government troops at 5:30 a.m. on November 6 and copies of the newspapers confiscated; by eleven o'clock that morning the newspapers reappeared. The government ordered the cruiser *Aurora,* manned by a Bolshevik crew and moored in the Neva uncomfortably close to the Winter Palace, to put to sea on a training cruise; the order was effectively countermanded by the Military Revolutionary Committee.

On the morning of the sixth, Kerensky appeared before the Pre-Parliament, proclaimed a state of insurrection in Petrograd, and asked for unqualified support in suppressing the Bolsheviks. After prolonged debate, with the Kadets and Cossack delegates in opposition, a resolution drafted by Martov, a Menshevik Internationalist, was adopted by the close vote of 113 to 102, with twenty-six abstentions. The resolution condemned the insurrection, but it pointed the finger of responsibility at Kerensky by calling on him "first of all, to pass immediately a decree transferring the land to the land committees and to take a decisive stand on foreign policy proposing to the Allies that they announce the conditions of peace and begin peace negotiations." The resolution concluded by recommending the creation of "a Committee of Public Safety comprised of representatives of municipal corporations and the organs of the revolutionary democracy, acting in concert with the Provisional Government."

Kerensky at first threatened to resign. A delegation headed by the Menshevik Dan called on the premier to plead for quick action in the spirit of the resolution. According to Dan's account,

[We told him] that we had a definite and concrete proposal to make to the Provisional Government: that resolutions on the question of peace, land, and the Constituent Assembly should be passed at once and made known to the population by means of telegraph and by posting bills [in the city]. We insisted that this must be done that very night in order that every soldier and every worker might know of the decisions of the Provisional Government by the next morning. . . .

We pleaded . . . with Kerensky that even from a purely military point of view the struggle against the Bolsheviks would have a chance of success only if the peasant-soldiers knew that they were defending peace and land against the Bolsheviks. . . .

Our conversation did not last very long. Kerensky gave the impression of a man completely enervated and worn out. To every argument he replied with irritation, saying finally with disdain that the government did not need any of our advice, that this was not the time to talk but to act.

THE SEIZURE OF POWER

Meanwhile, Lenin, still in hiding, had also decided that the moment had come for action. Burning with impatience, he sped a last letter to the comrades of the Central Committee of November 6: "We must not wait! We may lose everything! . . . History will not forgive delay by revolutionists who could be victorious today (and will surely be victorious today), while they risk losing much tomorrow, they risk losing all." Then, addressing himself to those who urged delay until the meeting of the Second All-Russian Congress of Soviets on the evening of the seventh, Lenin continued:

If we seize power today, we seize it not against the Soviets but for them. . . . The government is tottering. We must *deal it the death blow* at any cost. To delay action is the same as death.

On the same day, the Bolshevik Central Committee assembled to make the last dispositions for the uprising. Sverdlov was assigned to keep watch on the Provisional Government, Bubnov was allotted railway communications, Dzerzhinsky posts and telegraphs, and Milyutin the organization of food supplies. Kamenev and Berzin were instructed to negotiate with the Left SR's to insure their support for the insurrection. Lomov and Nogin were dispatched to Moscow to coordinate the activities of the Bolsheviks there. With events rushing toward a denouement, Trotsky took time out on the evening of the sixth to address a meeting of the Petrograd Soviet. In reporting on the measures already taken to checkmate the Provisional Government, he referrred to it "as nothing more than a pitiful, helpless, half-government, which waits the motion of a historical broom to sweep it off. . . . But if the government wishes to make use of the hours — 24, 48, or 72 — which it still has to live, and comes out against us, then we will meet it with a counterattack, blow for blow, steel for iron." During the night of the sixth and the early morning of the seventh, the Bolshevik forces moved quickly to seize the strong points of the capital city. Resistance was virtually nominal, and the seizures were accomplished with almost no bloodshed. The military support on which the Provisional Government counted simply melted away. A pathetic effort was made to hold the Winter Palace with the help of the Ural Cossacks, Junkers, officers, and Women's Battalion who were stationed there. But as the Bolsheviks moved up their forces, the Cossacks and part of the Junkers and officers slipped away, and the Women's Battalion was disarmed after sallying forth in counterattack. Shortly after midnight of the seventh, the attacking forces captured the last stronghold of the Provisional Gov-

ernment and arrested the ministers who remained in the Palace.

The collapse of resistance in Petrograd was complete. The proclamation of the Military Revolutionary Committee summed up the day's happenings:

All railroad stations and telephone, post, and telegraph offices are occupied. The telephones of the Winter Palace and the Staff Headquarters are disconnected. The State Bank is in our hands. The Winter Palace and the Staff have surrendered. The shock troops are dispersed, the cadets paralyzed. The armored cars have sided with the Revolutionary Committee. The Cossacks refused to obey the government. The Provisional Government is deposed. Power is in the hands of the Revolutionary Committee of the Petrograd Soviet of Workers' and Soldiers' Deputies.

At eleven o'clock on the evening of November 7, the Second All-Russian Congress of Soviets assembled for its opening session. Of the approximately 650 delegates in attendance, the Bolsheviks claimed 390 and with the help of the Left SR's quickly asserted control over the proceedings. Confronted with a *fait accompli*, the Mensheviks and SR's of the Right and Center abandoned the Congress. Martov, the Menshevik Internationalist whom Trotsky described contemptuously as the "inventive statesman of eternal waverings," attempted to patch up a truce by proposing "to end the crisis in a peaceful manner, by forming a government composed of representatives of all the democratic elements." Trotsky's reply was drenched in vitriol:

What do they offer us? . . . To give up our victory, to compromise, and to negotiate — with whom? With whom shall we negotiate? With those miserable cliques which have left the Congress or with those who still remain? But we saw how strong those cliques were! There is no one left in Russia to follow them. And millions of workers and peasants are asked to negotiate with them on equal terms. No, an agreement will not do now. To those who have left us and to those proposing negotiations we must say: You are a mere handful, miserable, bankrupt; your rôle is finished, and you may go where you belong — to the garbage heap of history.

The Congress concluded its first day's business by issuing a proclamation announcing its assumption of supreme power, transferring all local authority to the Soviets, and appealing to the country to defeat all efforts of Kerensky and other "Kornilovists" to return to power. With a sure revolutionary instinct for the issues that would attract maximum support for the Bolsheviks, the proclamation promised:

The Soviet authority will at once propose a democratic peace to all nations and an immediate armistice on all fronts. It will safeguard the transfer without compensation of all land ... to the peasant committees; it will defend the soldiers' rights, introducing a complete democratization of the army, it will establish workers' control over industry, it will insure the convocation of the Constituent Assembly on the date set; it will supply the cities with bread and the villages with articles of first necessity, and it will secure to all nationalities inhabiting Russia the right of self-determination.

The next day Lenin made his first appearance at the Congress and was received with a tumultuous ovation. After the applause had died down, he quickly assumed the reins of leadership with nine fateful words, "We shall now proceed to construct the socialist order." With Lenin presenting the main reports, the Congress approved the important decrees on peace and on land and then concluded its work by entrusting the power of government to the newly created Council of People's Commissars. The Sovnarkom, as it quickly became known, was exclusively Bolshevik in composition; its membership included Lenin as Chairman, Trotsky as Commissar of Foreign Affairs, Rykov as Commissar of the Interior, Lunacharsky as Commissar of Education, and Stalin as Chairman for Nationalities. The hour of triumph had finally come. Lenin rarely indulged in introspection or backward glances, but at that moment he paused in wonder and confided to Trotsky, "You know ... from persecution and a life underground, to come so suddenly into power ... *Es schwindelt.*"

If Lenin found victory intoxicating and slightly unbelievable, in the eyes of his opponents the Bolshevik march to power had a nightmarish quality of incredible unreality. In the brief period of eight months, a tiny band of underground revolutionaries, numbering less than 25,000 on the eve of the March Revolution, had catapulted themselves into a governing authority of nearly 150,000,000 people. It is easier to discern in retrospect the significant factors which contributed to the Bolshevik conquest than it was at the time. If the Provisional Government had been able to withdraw from the war and carry through a land settlement satisfactory to the peasantry, it is highly doubtful that the Bolsheviks could have gathered enough support to stage a successful *coup d'état.* Yet to state this alternative, so plausibly reinforced by hindsight, is to miss the tragic imperatives of 1917.

Each of the parties which maneuvered for ascendancy in the months between March and November was the prisoner of its own illusions, its own interests, and its own vision of the future. To a Kadet leader like Milyukov it was inconceivable that Russia could betray her allies and her own national interests by suing for a separate peace; consequently, it was all too easy to attribute his own sense of patriotic exaltation and dedication to soldiers, workers, and peasants who had lost their taste for war. To SR's of the Right like Kerensky, who in a measure shared Milyukov's illusions, the successful prosecution of the war was paramount, with the agenda of economic reforms to be postponed until properly constituted legal bodies could be assembled to deal with them. To SR's of the Center and Left, who were much closer to the aspirations and expectations of the villages, land reform brooked no delay. Frustrated by the procrastinations of the Provisional

Government, the Left SR's were thrown into the arms of the Bolsheviks. For Mensheviks of all shades, still loyal to the orthodox Marxian two-stage panorama of capitalist development, the socialist revolution had to be postponed until the bourgeois-democratic revolution was completed. The Mensheviks demonstrated real insight in emphasizing the difficulties of building socialism in a backward country. Their theoretical acumen was less well attuned to the political dynamism and revolutionary *élan* which the downfall of Tsardom released. For the Bolsheviks, economic backwardness was the springboard to power; for the Mensheviks, it pointed a path toward legal opposition in a consolidating bourgeois order. This was hardly a prospect for which the wretched and disinherited could develop more than qualified enthusiasm. As the Revolution deepened, the Mensheviks found themselves out-promised and out-maneuvered, with their strength sharply receding in the urban industrial centers on which they counted heavily.

Until the arrival of Lenin from exile, the Bolsheviks, too, were prisoners of ancient formulas. They oriented their policies on a perspective not very different from that of Menshevism. Lenin reversed this course and set the party on the road to the conquest of power. With an unswerving faith in his goal and a readiness to take any measures whatever to realize it, Lenin, frequently over bitter opposition, managed to transform the party into an obedient instrument of his will. His remarkable talent as a revolutionary strategist was based on an unerring sense for the deeply felt dissatisfactions of the masses and the genius for finding the slogans to catalyze grievances into revolutionary energy. Except for his insistence on striking at the right moment, Lenin had relatively little to do with the actual mechanics of the insurrection. His great contribution was to set the stage for insurrection by identifying Bolshevism with the major forces of mass discontent in Russian society. Lenin did not create the war-weariness which permeated the army and the nation:

the material was at hand; his task was to exploit it. With one word — peace — Lenin and the Bolsheviks fused it into a revolutionary amalgam. The land-hunger of the peasants was an ancient grievance of which all parties were aware. The SR's built their ascendancy in the villages on the promise to satisfy it, but while they temporized, Lenin stole their program from under their noses. When accused of the theft, Lenin replied, "Whether it be according to our ideas or in the direction of the SR program does not matter. The essential point is to give the peasantry a firm conviction that there are no more *pomeshchiks* [landlords] in the villages, and that it is now for the peasants themselves to solve all questions and to build their own life." With one word — land — Lenin insured the neutrality of the villages.

Factory workers constituted the strongest phalanx of Bolshevik support. Lenin bought their support by promising them a government which "takes surplus products from the parasites and gives them to the hungry, that . . . forcibly moves the homeless into the dwellings of the rich, that . . . forces the rich to pay for milk, but does not give them a drop of it until the children of *all* the poor families have received adequate supplies." With two slogans — bread and workers' control — Lenin captured the allegiance of substantial sections of the industrial workers from the Mensheviks.

The Bolshevik Revolution was not a majoritarian movement. The last free elections in Russia, the elections to the Constituent Assembly which took place toward the end of 1917, clearly demonstrated that the Bolshevik voting strength in the country at large was not more than 25 per cent. But, as Lenin subsequently observed, the Bolsheviks did have "an overwhelming preponderance of force at the decisive moment in the decisive points." In the areas and units strategically important to the success of the insurrection — Petrograd, Moscow, the Baltic fleet, and the garrisons around Petrograd — Bolshevik ascendancy turned the scale. The enemies of Bolshevism were numerous, but they were also weak, poorly organized, divided, and apathetic. The strategy of Lenin was calculated to emphasize their divisions, neutralize their opposition, and capitalize on their apathy. In 1902 in *What Is to Be Done?* Lenin had written, "Give us an organization of revolutionaries, and we shall overturn the whole of Russia!" On November 7, 1917, the wish was fulfilled and the deed accomplished.

Marxist-Leninist Theory Guided the Party

THE COMMUNIST PARTY OF THE SOVIET UNION

In general the *History of the Communist Party of the Soviet Union (Bolsheviks)* is an incredible distortion of known facts. It was published during the Stalin era when all Russian history was being rewritten to fit Stalin's demands. Famous men who played important roles are not mentioned; others are viciously maligned in order that the myth of Stalin as omniscient leader might remain inviolate. However, despite its glaring sins—and, to the scholar, deliberate falsification of the truth is one of the greatest of sins—this work is of immense significance. Since 1938 it has been the official truth about the revolution for millions of people in the Soviet Union and in other communist nations. It contains some of the most succinctly stated and widely read definitions of Marxist-Leninist theory that have ever been written. Until 1959 it was a sort of communist *Bible* used around the world, and indeed, its sales (some 50,-000,000 copies) outstripped those of the *Gospels* of the Christian faith. The following excerpt presents an important facet of the communist interpretation.

1. The history of the Party teaches us, first of all, that the victory of the proletarian revolution, the victory of the dictatorship of the proletariat, is impossible without a revolutionary party of the proletariat, a party free from opportunism, irreconcilable towards compromisers and capitulators, and revolutionary in its attitude towards the bourgeoisie and its state power.

The history of the Party teaches us that to leave the proletariat without such a party means to leave it without revolutionary leadership; and to leave it without revolutionary leadership means to ruin the cause of the proletarian revolution.

The history of the Party teaches us that the ordinary Social-Democratic Party of the West-European type, brought up under conditions of civil peace, trailing in the wake of the opportunists, dreaming of "social reforms," and dreading social revolution, cannot be such a party.

The history of the Party teaches us that only a party of the new type, a Marxist-Leninist party, a party of social revolution, a party capable of preparing the proletariat for decisive battles against the bourgeoisie and of organizing the victory of the proletarian revolution, can be such a party.

* * *

2. The history of the Party further teaches us that a party of the working class cannot perform the role of leader of its class, cannot perform the role of organizer and leader of the proletarian revolution, unless it has mastered the advanced theory of the working-class movement, the Marxist-Leninist theory.

The power of the Marxist-Leninist theory lies in the fact that it enables the Party to find the right orientation in any situation, to understand the inner connection of current events, to foresee their course and to perceive not only how and in what direction they are developing in the present, but how and in what direction they are bound to develop in the future.

From *History of the Communist Party of the Soviet Union (Bolsheviks)*, (New York, 1939), pp. 353, 355–58. By permission of International Publishers.

Only a party which has mastered the Marxist-Leninist theory can confidently advance and lead the working class forward.

On the other hand, a party which has not mastered the Marxist-Leninist theory is compelled to grope its way, loses confidence in its actions and is unable to lead the working class forward.

It may seem that all that is required for mastering the Marxist-Leninist theory is to diligently learn by heart isolated conclusions and propositions from the works of Marx, Engels and Lenin, learn to quote them at opportune times and rest at that, in hope that the conclusions and propositions thus memorized will suit each and every situation and occasion. But such an approach to the Marxist-Leninist theory is altogether wrong. The Marxist-Leninist theory must not be regarded as a collection of dogmas, as a catechism, as a symbol of faith, and the Marxists themselves as pedants and dogmatists. The Marxist-Leninist theory is the science of the development of society, the science of the working-class movement, the science of the proletarian revolution, the science of the building of the Communist society. And as a science it does not and cannot stand still, but develops and perfects itself. Clearly, in its development it is bound to become enriched by new experience and new knowledge, and some of its propositions and conclusions are bound to change in the course of time, are bound to be replaced by new conclusions and propositions corresponding to the new historical conditions.

Mastering the Marxist-Leninist theory does not at all mean learning all its formulas and conclusions by heart and clinging to their every letter. To master the Marxist-Leninist theory we must first of all learn to distinguish between its letter and substance.

Mastering the Marxist-Leninist theory means assimilating *the substance* of this theory and learning to use it in the solution of the practical problems of the revolutionary movement under the varying conditions of the class struggle of the proletariat.

Mastering the Marxist-Leninist theory means being able to enrich this theory with the new experience of the revolutionary movement, with new propositions and conclusions, it means being able to *develop it and advance it* without hesitating to replace — in accordance with the substance of the theory — such of its propositions and conclusions as have become antiquated by new ones corresponding to the new historical situation.

The Marxist-Leninist theory is not a dogma but a guide to action.

Before the second Russian revolution (February 1917), the Marxists of all countries assumed that the parliamentary democratic republic was the most suitable form of political organization of society in the period of transition from capitalism to Socialism. It is true that in the seventies Marx stated that the most suitable form for the dictatorship of the proletariat was a political organization of the type of the Paris Commune, and not the parliamentary republic. But, unfortunately, Marx did not develop this proposition any further in his writings and it was committed to oblivion. Moreover, Engels' authoritative statement in his criticism of the draft of the Erfurt Program in 1891, namely, that "the democratic republic . . . is . . . the specific form for the dictatorship of the proletariat" left no doubt that the Marxists continued to regard the democratic republic as the political form for the dictatorship of the proletariat. Engels' proposition later became a guiding principle for all Marxists, including Lenin. However, the Russian Revolution of 1905, and especially the Revolution of February 1917, advanced a new form of political organization of society — the Soviets of Workers' and Peasants' Deputies. As a result of a study of the experience of the two Russian revolutions, Lenin, on the basis of the theory of Marxism, arrived at the conclusion that the best political form for the dictatorship of the proletariat was not a parliamentary democratic republic, but a republic of Soviets. Proceeding from this, Lenin, in April 1917, during the period of transition from the bourgeois to the Socialist revolution, issued the slogan of a republic of Soviets as the best political form for the dictatorship of the proletariat. The opportunists of all countries clung to the parliamentary republic and accused Lenin of departing from Marxism and destroying democracy. But it was Lenin, of course, who was the real Marxist who had mastered the theory of Marxism, and not the opportunists, for Lenin was advancing the Marxist theory by enriching it with new experience, whereas the opportunists were dragging it back and transforming one of its propositions into a dogma.

What would have happened to the Party, to our revolution, to Marxism, if Lenin had been overawed by the letter of Marxism and had not had the courage to replace one of the old propositions of Marxism, formulated by Engels, by the new proposition regarding the republic of Soviets, a proposition that corresponded to the new historical conditions? The Party would have groped in the dark, the Soviets would have been disorganized, we should not have had a Soviet power, and the Marxist theory would have suffered a severe setback. The proletariat would have lost, and the enemies of the proletariat would have won.

As a result of a study of pre-imperialist capitalism Engels and Marx arrived at the conclusion that the Socialist revolution could not be victorious in one country, taken singly, that it could be victorious only by a simultaneous stroke in all, or the majority of the civilized countries. That was in the middle of the nineteenth century. This conclusion later became a guiding principle for all Marxists. However, by the beginning of the twentieth century, pre-imperialist capitalism had grown into imperialist capitalism, ascendant capitalism had turned into moribund capitalism. As a result of a study of imperialist capitalism, Lenin, on the basis of the Marxist theory, arrived at the conclusion that the old formula of Engels and Marx no longer corresponded to the new historical conditions, and that the victory of the Socialist

revolution was quite possible in one country, taken singly. The opportunists of all countries clung to the old formula of Engels and Marx and accused Lenin of departing from Marxism. But it was Lenin, of course, who was the real Marxist who had mastered the theory of Marxism, and not the opportunists, for Lenin was advancing the Marxist theory by enriching it with new experience, whereas the opportunists were dragging it back, mummifying it.

What would have happened to the Party, to our revolution, to Marxism, if Lenin had been overawed by the letter of Marxism and had not had the courage of theoretical conviction to discard one of the old conclusions of Marxism and to replace it by a new conclusion affirming that the victory of Socialism in one country, taken singly, was possible, a conclusion which corresponded to the new historical conditions? The Party would have groped in the dark, the proletarian revolution would have been deprived of leadership, and the Marxist theory would have begun to decay. The proletariat would have lost, and the enemies of the proletariat would have won.

Opportunism does not always mean a direct denial of the Marxist theory or of any of its propositions and conclusions. Opportunism is sometimes expressed in the attempt to cling to certain of the propositions of Marxism that have already become antiquated and to convert them into a dogma, so as to retard the further development of Marxism, and, consequently, to retard the development of the revolutionary movement of the proletariat.

It may be said without fear of exaggeration that since the death of Engels the master theoretician Lenin, and after Lenin, Stalin and the other disciples of Lenin, have been the only Marxists who have advanced the Marxist theory and who have enriched it with new experience in the new conditions of the class struggle of the proletariat.

And just because Lenin and the Leninists have advanced the Marxist theory, Leninism is a further development of Marxism; it is Marxism in the new conditions of the class struggle of the proletariat, Marxism of the epoch of imperialism and proletarian revolutions, Marxism of the epoch of the victory of Socialism on one-sixth of the earth's surface.

The Bolshevik Party could not have won in October 1917 if its foremost men had not mastered the theory of Marxism, if they had not learned to regard this theory as a guide to action, if they had not learned to advance the Marxist theory by enriching it with the new experience of the class struggle of the proletariat.

SUGGESTIONS FOR ADDITIONAL READING

The chief purpose of this bibliographical note is to provide a very small list of some of the most interesting and useful works on the revolution available in English. More extensive bibliographies are available in Philip Grierson's *Books on Soviet Russia, 1917–1924* (London, 1943) and in the supplements to this work published later in *The Slavonic and East European Review*. Annual listings of books and articles on the Soviet Union are also published in *The Russian Review*.

Some of the best general accounts (Chamberlin, Trotsky, and Chernov) have been excerpted in this book. However, there are several others which have much to offer. Bertram Wolfe's *Three Who Made a Revolution* (Boston, 1948) makes an eloquent and fascinating introduction to the development of Marxist revolutionary thought and organization in the years leading up to 1914. *The Fall of the Russian Monarchy* by Sir Bernard Pares (London, 1939) is a moving account of the monarchy from the beginning of the 20th century to the Tsar's abdication and death; its overemphasis on politics and court life may be balanced by reading Michael T. Florinsky's *The End of the Russian Empire* (New Haven, 1931). The last ten chapters of the Florinsky book, *Russia, A History and an Interpretation* (New York, 1953), is an over-all account which makes exhaustive use of recent monographic literature. The several volumes of *The Bolshevik Revolution, 1917–1923* (New York, 1951–1953) by E. H. Carr are quite useful where they actually touch upon the events prior to November, 1917, but for the most part these volumes deal with the years after the revolution. Of particular value for an understanding of the peasant, his problems, and his perception of the revolution is the book by Sir John Maynard, *Russia in Flux* (New York, 1949); the useful but more specialized work by Launcelot Owen, *The Russian Peasant Movement, 1906–1917*

(London, 1937), places much of its attention upon agrarian events between March and October of 1917.

There are many richly informative eye-witness reports. One of the best, a classic in the field, is *Ten Days That Shook the World* (New York, 1935) by John Reed. Reed was an extremely talented young American journalist with a flair for being at the right place in Petrograd during 1917 and a burning enthusiasm for the Bolsheviks. *Raymond Robin's Own Story* (New York, 1920) by W. Hard recounts the experiences of an American colonel of the Red Cross who through the second half of 1917 had close contacts with the revolutionary governments. Two ambassadors have written superior memoirs. In *My Mission to Russia and Other Diplomatic Memories* (2 vols., London and Boston, 1923), Sir George Buchanan reports his conversations with the Emperor; and in *An Ambassador's Memoirs* (3 vols., London, 1923–1925) Maurice Paléologue of France provides penetrating and thoughtful analyses of the political and social decadence of the Imperial regime. Of the numerous accounts by Russians it is almost impossible to select the best, but among the first of these is the work by N. N. Sukhanov, *The Russian Revolution, 1917* (London, 1955). Alexander Kerensky's *The Prelude to Bolshevism: The Kornilov Rebellion* (London, 1919) and *The Catastrophe* (New York and London, 1927) are prejudiced but valuable. *Survival Through War and Revolution* (London and New York, 1939) by Dmitry Fedotoff White is a naval officer's description of events in the fleet at Petrograd in 1917 which gives a fine flavor of the revolutionary temper of the Bolshevik sailors.

It is, of course, quite impossible to understand the revolution without knowing a great deal about Lenin and his special variation of Marxism, subjects best learned by studying the pre-1917 development of the man and the theory. Of the immense literature that has grown up around these topics, the book by Wolfe mentioned above is a lively and very human account. Leopold Haimson's admirable book, *The Russian Marxists and the Origins of Bolshevism* (Cambridge, Mass., 1955) is a brilliant and penetrating study of the development of Marxism into Leninism, which unfortunately ends at 1905. Alfred G. Meyer's *Leninism* (Cambridge, Mass., 1957) is one of the best scholarly monographs available and is essential reading. The uneven volumes published as V. I. Lenin's *Collected Works* (New York, 1927–1932) represent six volumes of the Russian editions; volumes XX and XXI present his speeches, letters, and articles of 1917 and graphically depict his frame of mind and his analysis of events during the crucial months of the struggle for power. The somewhat overcritical but exhaustive study by Oliver H. Radkey, *The Agrarian Foes of Bolshevism* (New York, 1958) is a much-needed history of the trials and tribulations of Lenin's Socialist Revolutionary opponents.

Far too many biographical works written about the men involved in the revolution have been too superficial or biased to be of real worth. Isaac Deutscher's study of Stalin and *The Prophet Armed: Trotsky, 1879–1921* (London and New York, 1954) are both authoritative and readable. The biographies of Lenin tend to adulate or condemn. The best of these, David Shub's *Lenin: A Biography* (New York, 1948), while useful, does not go very deep and tends to emphasize the sensational. One of the mysteries that every student must try to solve for himself is the question of Rasputin's significance for Russia. *The Reign of Rasputin: An Empire's Collapse* (London, 1927) by the former president of the Duma, M. V. Rodzianko, is an unbalanced account by a man obsessed with hatred for Rasputin, but it very clearly points up Rasputin's malevolent influence. *Rasputin, the Holy Devil* (New York, 1929) by René Fülop-Miller contains documentary evidence concerning Rasputin's almost unbelievable personal character. No better picture of Rasputin's influence or of the characters of Emperor Nicholas II and his wife Alexandra can ever be drawn than that which they have sketched themselves in *Letters of the Tsaritsa to the Tsar, 1914–1916* (introd. by Sir Bernard Pares, London, 1923) and *The Letters of the Tsar to the Tsaritsa, 1914–1917* (introd. by C. T. Hagberg Wright, London, 1929).

The foreign affairs of Russia in 1917 and their influence upon the internal situation are described by Robert D. Warth in *The Allies and the Russian Revolution* (Durham, N. C., 1954), which strongly supports the thesis that had there been no Kornilov revolt the Provisional Government might have been more successful against the Bolsheviks. A very full bibliography of secondary and source materials in English makes this book especially useful for the student investigating this special area.

The importance of the nationalities movements, which has too often been missed by writers who tend to see only the dramatic events in Petrograd and Moscow, is clearly delineated by Richard Pipes in his *The Formation of the Soviet Union: Communism and Nationalism, 1917–1923* (Cambridge, Mass., 1954). *The Ukrainian Revolution, 1917–1920* (Princeton, 1952) by John Reshetar, Jr., is an authoritative monograph which develops in detail the revolutionary activity of one such minority movement; a similar study of another area is *The Struggle for Transcaucasia, 1917–1921* (New York, 1951) by Firuz Kazemzadeh.

Among the standard documentary collections two are of major value. *The Bolshevik Revolution, 1917–1918* (edited by James Bunyan and H. H. Fisher, Stanford, 1934) contains a mass of materials ranging from excerpted memoirs and personal statements by the participants to the records and orders of government and party officials. *Documents on Russian History, 1914–1917* (New York, 1927) by Frank A. Golder is of similar value.